Praise for Clark Finnical

Praise for *Job Hunting Secrets (from someone who's been there)*

This book is both pragmatic and inspiring. It empowers job searchers, as though they have a knowledgeable friend walking with them every step of the way. It answers the key questions in the job hunt for the 21st century. Highly recommended!

Jim Wylde, *Director, Career and Graduate Student Services, Elliott School of International Affairs, George Washington University*

I've never seen a book as thorough, well-researched, and helpful as this one. Clark Finnical has done an outstanding job in offering sound, practical, and detailed advice to job-hunters.

Christopher Largent, *Widener University Law School Lecturer, University of Delaware Adjunct Professor and Director of the Seventh Academy*

Practical, easy to navigate and hits all the big job-hunting traps to avoid. You'll find sections on making your resume easy to read to getting through those frustrating applicant tracking systems to tips on how to get comfortable bragging about yourself in an interview and much more.

Kerry Hannon, *Author of Great Jobs for Everyone 50+, What's Next? Follow Your Passion and Find Your Dream Job, Getting the Job You Want After 50 For Dummies*

This book is a thorough overview of what job hunters encounter. Included are sections on increasing your chances for finding a job, resume writing, interviewing, what employers look for in applicants, overcoming feeling alone/isolated in a job search, differentiating yourself from other candidates, and more.

Wyn Bumgardner, *CEO, Career-Locator*

1

The book is extremely thorough...You can tell the author has walked a mile, or five, in a job seeker's shoes because this book truly thinks of everything.

Kristin A. Sherry, *Author of YouMap: Find Yourself. Blaze Your Path. Show the World!, 5 Surprising Steps to Land the Job NOW! & Follow Your Star: Career Lessons I Learned from Mom*

This is a practical approach to getting a job you love...You get an idea of what is truly going on, how to navigate past the common barriers, and seal the deal in your quest to gain better employment.

Taylor Tagg, *Co-founder of Journey to Success Podcast & Radio Network*

Read the book for yourself for a treasure trove of information written by someone who successfully navigated the complicated job search process and now generously shares his wisdom.

Patricia Edwards, *Former Talent Manager & HR Business Leader*

Excellent book. It is an easy to read reference guide from someone who has first-hand experience looking for a job and the way to overcome the pitfalls and frustrations of conducting today's job search. As a career coach, I will recommend this book to my clients.

Raymond Gooch, *Career Coach & Founder of Job Search That Works Podcast*

Excellent Read. Succinct, well written and applicable to those who are new to the workforce or those who need a refresher.

Jason Hill, *CEO of Parallon Business Solutions, Tampa*

This book is so effective it almost feels like cheating! Clark might as well be sitting right beside you as co-pilot with its easy layout and conversational style, guiding you, the reader to look at your own mindset before helping you to quantify personal achievements, to putting it on paper, to the important follow through with effective networking tips and psychology.

Liam Parfitt, *Regional Manager, Supreme Court of Newfoundland and Labrador & Graduate of Cambridge University*

I've been in a job elimination situation and wish I would have had this book then. It's written so someone seeking their first job or someone who has to jump back into the job seeker market can benefit from this. I wholeheartedly recommend this book.

Kathy Burkhardt, *Regional Director of Health Information, Parallon Business Solutions, West Florida*

Great book!! Very detailed but ALSO very easy to follow. I have worked with a number of Fortune 500 companies in my 20+ years in advertising and 'Job Hunting Secrets' is a perfect roadmap for both college grads as well those further along and looking to make a career change.

Scott Mullins, *CEO of Mind Design Group Inc*

This book serves as a thorough guide for achieving success in the job market! It's applicable to all seeking employment and would serve as an excellent gift to someone graduating and moving into the workforce.

Peter Benaquisto, *Director of Payroll, Parallon Business Solutions, Tampa*

An extremely easy-to-read, practical and valuable tool to help anyone searching for a job! Clark Finnical writes from the perspective of one who has learned job hunting skills from being "in the trenches". The tips on improving my LinkedIn profile helped me land the job I have today.

Glenn Cate, *Wireless Network Engineer, Tech Data & Founder of the Wi-Fi Blogroll*

I love this book so much that I just picked up a 2nd copy of it so that I can send the first one I have to a friend who is on a job hunt of her own. It's a must read for all job seekers!

Barbara Bermudez, *Manager of Transcription, Parallon Business Solutions, Tampa*

Additional Books Written by Clark Finnical

Job Hunting Secrets (from someone who's been there)

LinkedIn Strategies to Take Your Career to the Next Level

Written by Job Search Veteran and Job Seeker Advocate

Clark Finnical

IMPORTANT DISCLAIMER

Ordering Information

Quantity sales: Special discounts are available on quantity purchases by colleges, universities, associations and others. For details contact the publisher at the address above.

ISBN: 9781724033574

LinkedIn Strategies to Take Your Career to the Next Level

Written by Job Search Veteran and Job Seeker Advocate

Clark Finnical

1. Job Hunting. 2. Careers. 3. Self-Help. 4. LinkedIn. 5. Business.

The stories about the people in the book do not use their actual names.

Copyright Page

Dedication

To HB, without her patience, love and support, this book would never have been written.

Table of Contents

Foreword

I joined LinkedIn in January 2009. My first connection was my husband. (Only he wasn't my husband at the time...Yet).

In my first year on LinkedIn, I had less than 30 connections and no followers.

In 2010, I added 24 connections, with 99% of them working at the same company as me.

In 2011, I added 8 connections.

In 2012, I added zero.

2013 was a big year. 200 connections added!

There I was, with just under 300 connections.

In 2014, everything changed. I decided to start paying attention to LinkedIn to see what it was all about, perhaps meet some people, read some content, comment on people's posts, and contribute some content of my own.

By the end of 2015, I had about 1,000 connections and gained an additional 6,000 followers of my content.

Today, I add about 1,000 followers monthly writing content on LinkedIn which has opened doors for me I could never have opened without it.

Because of LinkedIn, I wrote the foreword of Dawn Metcalfe's book, The HardTalk Handbook. Dawn is based in Dubai and I never would have met her if not for LinkedIn.

Because of LinkedIn, I was able to meet amazing resume and LinkedIn profile writers like Kerri Twigg, Patricia Edwards, Lisa Jones, Kamara Toffolo, and Donna Serdula, and I invited all of them to contribute to my most recent book.

LinkedIn can open doors for you, too. And Clark Finnical is just the person to show you how. His passionate advocacy for job seekers is unparalleled.

I connected with Clark on LinkedIn on March 13, 2017 at 6:44 PM and through our interactions on LinkedIn he has now presented me the honor of writing the foreword to LinkedIn Strategies to Take Your Career to the Next Level.

How did I know all of this information I've just presented to you? I learned how to access the data in this very book. Clark will show you how to use it to do something much more valuable – to land a new job.

You will get out of LinkedIn what you put into it, and LinkedIn Strategies to Take Your Career to the Next Level provides insider tips that I guarantee most LinkedIn users don't know.

LinkedIn has been a gamer changer for me. It can be for you, too.

God's blessings for your success!

Kristin Sherry, author of YouMap: Find Yourself. Blaze Your Path. Show the World!, 5 Surprising Steps to Land the Job NOW! and Follow Your Star: Career Lessons I Learned from Mom.

Charlotte, North Carolina, October 2018

Your Vision...

Job seeking is one of the hardest things you will ever do. Without a vision as to how you will do it, the entire process can be frustrating, discouraging and, sometimes even depressing.

Between 1989 and 2013, I was in the job market 5 times. Yes, it sucked, however I was able to work through those times, because I believed I was going to land work.

I followed what Saint Augustin said, namely:

"Pray as if everything depends on God

and work as if everything depends on you."

As a result, I woke up every morning, prayed to God and, kept 'plugging away.' Okay, I had my down moments, but when I did, I called someone, talked and was able to move on and keep plugging.

Sometimes this meant **applying for positions**.

Other times it meant **calling hiring managers** and expressing my interest in the role.

Still, other times, it meant **emailing decision-makers,** to let them know I was available, as they considered, their future staffing needs. I also provided a quick summary of my strengths and recommendations, from past supervisors, in that email.

Because, I knew I had to make an open and shut case, as to why *I* should be selected over others, **I created detailed achievement stories,** where I explained the obstacles I overcame and the problems I solved. Because nothing speaks louder than numbers, my stories included the money I earned for the company, the money I saved for the company, how I enhanced productivity and how I made a positive difference.[1]

Since it's not easy for a hiring manager to decide why she should choose one candidate over another, I created a portfolio that contained recommendations from prior supervisors and co-workers, recognition, awards, achievement stories, references and, work examples.[2]

Because, I knew I had to understand how the hiring manager thinks, I purchased Don Georgevich's Interview Questions and Answers. Don's material helped me to better understand what is running through a hiring manager's mind. In addition, I learned the questions I need to ask, to see if the hiring manager has any concerns about my ability to do the job.

Where do you stand?

"Do you believe you'll be hired?"

If you don't think what you believe matters or, even if you never thought about what you believe...

Consider what Cynthia Shapiro said, in her wonderful book, *What Does Somebody Have to Do to Get A Job Around Here?*

> *"What you're telling yourself with your inner voice*
> *comes through in every stage of your job search process."*

When you have negative or insecure self-talk, constantly running through your head, it will tend to govern the tone of your cover letters, e-mails, phone screenings and interviews.

Cynthia shared how successful athletes visualize getting baskets, making touchdowns, or hitting home runs.

As job seekers, we need to do the same thing. We need to visualize succeeding in interviews, excitedly sharing our achievement stories and enjoying getting to know the hiring managers and their teams.

Carrie Krueger, Vice President of Jobfully said:

> *"When you apply for a job, you are asking a prospective employer to believe in you. That leap of faith will be much more likely if you believe in yourself."*

Self-belief is critical to your job search. It creates a confidence that comes through in every encounter, allowing you to effectively sell yourself and get hired.

"So, do you believe you'll be hired?"

If you don't believe you'll be hired...

Stop everything you're doing and ask yourself why.

It could be you're selling yourself short and you're underestimating your God-given abilities.

It could be you're listening to the wrong folks. There will always be people who will put you down. Get as far away from these people as you can. If you cannot get far away, turn up the volume on your ear buds, so you can't hear them anymore!

It could also be you're pursuing the wrong roles; roles that really weren't meant for you.

If you're pursuing the wrong roles, positions or jobs consider the words of cartoonist Cathy Guisewite:

"Take the classes, the friends, and the family that have inspired the most in you. Save them in your permanent memory and make a backup disk. When you remember what you love, you will remember who you are. If you remember who you are, you can do anything."

I can help you AFTER you've decided on the type of job you want to pursue. If you haven't decided, consider reading one or more of these books:

What Color Is Your Parachute? by Richard Bolles, has sold more than 10,000,000 copies since its first publication. It is rewritten every year, and has been translated into 20 languages and published in 26 countries.

The book is more than job seeking as you can see in these chapters:

- Self-Inventory Parts 1 & 2;
- The Five Ways to Choose / Change Careers;
- How to Start Your Own Business;

- Finding Your Mission in Life;

- A Guide to Choosing a Career Coach or Counselor.

The Pathfinder by Nicholas Lore uses the techniques of the Rockport Institute, Lore's career-guidance network, to make *The Pathfinder* a substitute for a job counselor. Through goal setting, list making, and other techniques, the book leads readers through deciding exactly what they want to do for a living and finding a way to make it happen.

The book consists of three parts:

- Living A Life You Love;

- How to Get There from Here;

- Designing Your Future Career.

Do What You Are is written by Barbara Barron and Kelly Tieger. Richard Bolles, author of *What Color is Your Parachute?* says:

"This is one of the most popular career books in the world. It's easy to see why. Many have found great help from the concept of Personality Type, and Tieger and Barron are masters at explaining this approach to career choice. Highly recommended."

The authors broke the book into three sections:

- Part One – Unlocking the Secrets of Personality Type;

- Part Two – The 'Formula' for Career Satisfaction;

- Part Three – Getting to Work.

Part Three has a chapter on each Myers-Briggs Personality Type, where it discusses the type of work preferred by each of those personality types.

As I said before, self-belief is critical to your job search. It creates a confidence that comes through in every encounter, allowing you to effectively sell yourself and get hired!

"If you believe you'll be hired, please continue reading…"

How This Book Will Help You

I wrote this book so you will understand how to use LinkedIn to land work and get back to your normal everyday life.

Today's job seeking world benefits those who play in that world every day, namely the Recruiters, HR managers and Hiring Managers.

As a result, there are a lot of myths, misconceptions and sometimes, downright lies that put the job seeker at a disadvantage.[1]

This book was written to level that playing field, because you deserve a better job search experience than mine.

I never felt anyone was looking out for job seekers. That's why I wrote this book and that's why I've created, 'The Job Seeker's Advocate LLC.'

Because of my experiences, I understand what you're going through in a way other's who haven't been job seekers will never understand.

I was in the job market 5 times.

1. In 1989, my final year at school, I sent 60 resumes out. Most employers didn't respond. Those who did sent rejection letters. I didn't know what would happen until an on-campus interview. Thankfully the Recruiter was impressed, and I was ultimately hired.

2. In 1995, my division was put up for sale. We were told most of our jobs would eventually be eliminated. Some lost jobs immediately. Thankfully, I didn't. After scanning the corporate jobs system, I found the perfect match in another division and won over that hiring manager.

3. In 2002, this division restructured. My boss and I, along with many others lost their jobs. I went off payroll. I had no idea what the future held. One Friday afternoon my old employer called. They needed my social security number. Only then, did I learn an interview two weeks earlier, had converted into a job.

4. In 2010, during the Great Recession, everyone in my division from the Senior Vice-President to my boss lost their jobs over a 12-months period. I was off payroll for almost 6 months!

Thankfully, God gave me the smarts to get referrals that led to interviews and a great job in a great department.

5. In 2012, when the recession combined with a shrinking market for my employer's products, my job was eliminated again. I spoke to 100 people, but there was no future for me there. Fortunately, a retirement package eased the transition.

With my employer of 24 years out of the picture, I applied for jobs in sunny Florida. After not getting any bites I relocated to Florida, assuming my out-of-state residence was the reason Florida based employers hadn't responded to my applications. It wasn't.

In fact, it was not until I started working six months later as a short-term contractor that I started getting bites. Thankfully, my contract was renewed, twice! During that time, I interviewed with a well-run company, where I still work now, almost five years later!

In short, I'm one of you. Even though I'm happily employed today, I understand what you are feeling, thinking and, experiencing because of what I've been through.

Why LinkedIn Matters

1.) My LinkedIn profile has played an instrumental role in my career, as it can in yours.

2.) There are so many things you can do with LinkedIn, which will help you in your career, you'll wish you had read this book earlier and you may even share it with your friends.

LinkedIn can help you, but only if you know *how* to use it!

Some people sign up for LinkedIn and think that is all they have to do.

If this is you, I strongly recommend reading further.

Why Should You Go to All of This Effort?

Some of you might be thinking, "Why do I have to go to all of this trouble?" Here's why:

1. To increase your likelihood of being found by Recruiters;

2. To win over Recruiters and Hiring Managers by explaining as thoroughly as possible why you would be a valuable employee.

The Obstacle and the Opportunity

If you go to LinkedIn's news site and click through to their statistics page, you'll find as of 2018, there are more than 575,000,000 registered members on LinkedIn.[1]

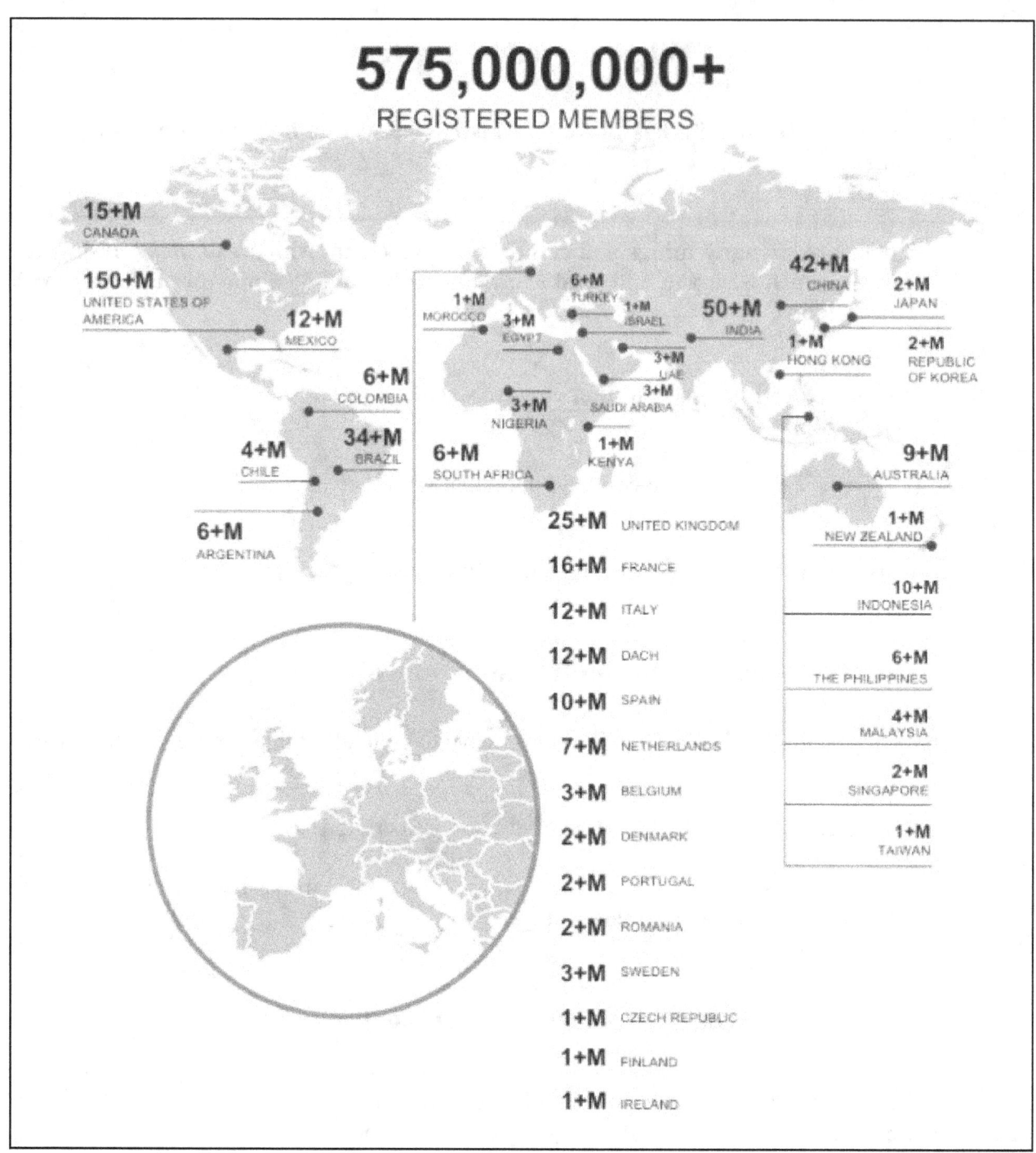

So, the obstacle is the other 575,000,000 LinkedIn members preventing you from being found.

The opportunity is that among those 575,000,000 LinkedIn members, are recruiters and hiring managers who need your skills.

Studies show recruiters spend about 6 seconds before they make the initial 'fit/no fit' decision on a LinkedIn profile.[2]

But, before recruiters can decide where you fit, they need to find you!

In the next section, I'm going to show you what I did to be found when I was in the job market.

Of course, getting found is not enough to land that interview. I'm also going to show you exactly what I did, so recruiters called me. Namely, what I did to demonstrate how I am different from other candidates.

I'm going to explain and show you how you can do the same thing.

Read This Warning Before Going On!

If you know anything about human nature, you'll understand the quote below:

"New opinions are always suspected and usually opposed because they are not already common."

~ John Locke

In other words, if people haven't heard something in the past, they'll question it. What these folks are not considering is new things are always coming around the corner, particularly these days.

I share this warning because when you tell others what you've learned from reading my book, don't be taken aback if you hear, "I've never heard that before."

If you hear those words, you can tell them:

"I'm not surprised you've never heard words like these because HR veterans and recruiters were the only people writing books for job seekers in the past.

'LinkedIn Strategies to Take Your Career to The Next Level' was written by someone like me — someone whose job was eliminated, someone who adapted to his new circumstances and did what he had to do to land work.

He's been through this more times than he'd like to remember. However, because of his desire to learn all he can about the job search experience, I now have a book on conducting a successful job search written by someone who's been in my shoes, someone who knows exactly what I'm going through, someone who knows exactly what I'm thinking, someone who knows exactly what I'm feeling and, most importantly, someone who has done everything possible to help job seekers understand how to land work."

Don't get me wrong. I'm not trying to minimize the value of books written by HR veterans and recruiters. In fact, as you read my book, you'll see I've included some of their valuable insights!

Before Doing Anything to Your LinkedIn Profile...

How to Avoid Irritating Your Connections

One of the best ways to avoid irritating your LinkedIn connections is to turn off the Profile Update notifications, before you start updating your profile.

If you don't do this and, you proceed to make all of the changes we'll discuss below, they will receive a sudden, violent and copious outpouring of notifications that will test the depth and strength of your relationships!

You don't want your connections to think about disconnecting and you don't want to 'bug' your friends.

Here is how to prevent this problem from ever occurring:

Click on the small round version of your profile photo where it says, 'Me' at the top of the LinkedIn site > Select 'Settings & Privacy'

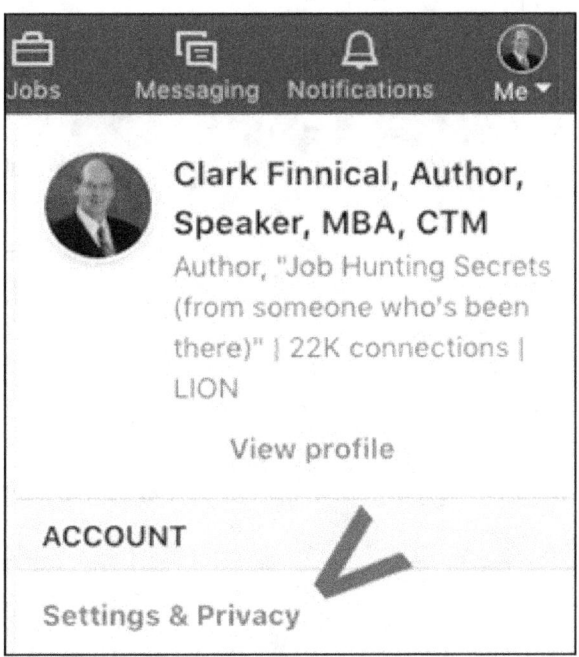

Select 'Privacy'> Scroll down to 'Sharing Profile Edits' > Click 'Sharing Profile Edits' or 'Change' (both will work) > Click 'No' > Click 'Close.'

Privacy	Ads	Communications

Choose who can see when you are on LinkedIn

Sharing profile edits   Close

Choose whether your network is notified about profile changes   No

Do you want to share your profile changes with your network? Your network may see when you change your profile, make recommendations, or follow companies.

No ⬤

How I Got the Recruiter's Attention

"If I can't find you, you don't exist."

~ Recruiter

Keywords Are Recruiter Magnets

Recruiters are paid to fill the needs of their corporate clients.

Just shy of 100%, of all recruiters use LinkedIn.

But, at 575,000,000+ members, recruiters would go homeless if they simply browsed through LinkedIn.

They use advanced search techniques called 'Boolean searches.'

Because the role of a Financial Analyst can sometimes be listed as 'Finance Analyst' or 'Financial Analyst' or 'Reports Analyst' or 'Sales Analyst' or 'Forecast Analyst', ad infinitum, they're going to search for 'Analyst.'

Because, I wanted to be at the top of the recruiter's search results, I had to find a way to include as many instances of 'Analyst' in my profile as possible.

So instead of putting 4-5 bullets under each position, I expanded the description to include all of my roles.

Expanding requires thinking differently. Once we create a resume, it's easy to think our resume contains all of our accomplishments.

When we think this way, we are forgetting about the very meaning of the word 'resume.' The term 'resume' comes from the French verb, 'resumer,' which means to sum up.

The noun, 'resume' is related to the verb, 'summarize,' which dictionary.com defines as 'to state or express in a concise form.'

With that understanding, it is crystal clear why my resume included this brief account of my experience as a 'Business Analyst.'

Business Analyst, Services Offer Management (2002–2010)
Drove three corporate internal audits, and their IT projects to closure, supported Six Sigma and Kaizen initiatives, identified and implemented new practices and processes for ending services support on legacy equipment, created business process improvements.

- Added $7.2M to the bottom line and preserved $5.4M by analyzing offer creation and sunset processes and implementing corrective measures.
- Generated $2M in billings by leading cross functional initiative to correct under-billing of 5000 customers while reducing billing failure rate by > 50%.
- Project managed development / delivery of training materials for new Indian team while interviewing job applicants, providing on-site training and on-going mentoring.
- Created new reporting leading to improved decision-making: Operations Review highlighting financial and operations results for executives, Monthly Portfolio Revenue reports for Offer Managers and maintenance contract reports.
- Enhanced Associate productivity by documenting 500+ pages of job aids explaining how to create reports by retrieving business critical data from SAP and other systems.

Your LinkedIn profile is an altogether different animal. There is no one or two-page limit. As a result, there is NO need to be brief. There is NO need to summarize. There is NO need to be concise!

In fact, any attempt to be concise in your LinkedIn profile will make it harder for you to be found. Any attempt to be brief in your LinkedIn profile will also result in your selling yourself short.

You will be selling yourself short because you will have denied yourself the opportunity to fully explain everything you've accomplished.

Adding Keywords to the Experience Section

By thinking differently, I was able to add the keyword 'Analyst' five times. By thinking differently, I was also able to list 14 separate accomplishments versus the five bullet points above.

Business **Analyst** | Financial **Analyst** | Business Operations

Oct 2002 – Oct 2010 • 8 yrs 1 mo

BEFORE: Offer Creation process flawed.
AFTER: Analysis revealed misconfigured offers; worked with other departments to correct errors. Recognized $7.2M. Implemented process to prevent future errors.

BEFORE: Offer Discontinuance Approval process broken.
AFTER: Analysis revealed manager discontinued active offers generating $5.4M annually. Created reporting enabling product managers to see financial impact of their decisions.

BEFORE: Analysis identified 5000 under-billed Maintenance customers. Existing processes flawed.
AFTER: Worked with others through an analysis of the problem resulting in developing systematic solutions. $2M generated as 5000 customers' billing corrected; Billing failure rate cut by 50%; Two internal audit items and corresponding IT projects successfully driven to closure.

BEFORE: Ending Services Support on legacy products very time consuming.
AFTER: Analysis of the process and teaming with another SME resulting in a time-based project management tool enabling managers to know what to do, when to do it and who to work with.

BEFORE: Expertise to generate business critical data limited to small number of Associates.
AFTER: As a Business **Analyst**, I created 500+ pages of job aids enabling others to retrieve business critical data. Documentation analysis ensured that even novices could quickly get up to speed.

Lean | Kaizen | Six Sigma Specialist

Jan 2007 – Sep 2010 • 3 yrs 9 mos

> Supported Director in Kaizen through ongoing research and analysis; he said, "Your help was invaluable to this team in terms of the questions you helped answer and the policy documents you helped develop and shared."

> Received Ovation Award for my role in the Six Sigma project which resulted in improvements in the SKU implementation process.

> Supported Senior Manager in the Customer for Life Six Sigma project which made the first significant steps to document the ending services support process.

Project Manager | **Analyst**

Jan 2006 – Aug 2010 • 4 yrs 8 mos

> > Development / delivery of training for Indian Offer Management Team. Delivered materials a week ahead of schedule.

> > Cross-departmental team responsible for resolving under-billing of 5000 customers.

> > Three audit-driven corporate IT initiatives from an analysis and writing of the business requirements to User Acceptance Testing and implementation.

Reporting **Analyst**

Oct 2002 – Jul 2010 • 7 yrs 10 mos

> Created quarterly Global Maintenance Operations Review for executive consumption; Analysis identified key revenue, margin and business performance metrics that will be of interest to Leadership.

> Product managers could not tell if their portfolio's were successful; analysis of a Finance-sanctioned report determined that it could be used to produce monthly portfolio revenue reporting.

> Provided business-critical data as needed to support management decision-making; on-going analysis enabled me to act as a consultant to Leadership who could explain the "so what" of the business-critical data.

In fact, I did this with all my roles.

Pricing **Analyst** | Operations **Analyst**

Jan 1999 – Oct 2002 • 3 yrs 10 mos

BEFORE: We were losing a large number of deals and did not know why.
AFTER: Analysis of Special Bids tool identified erroneous cost data. Created Special Bids tool with accurate cost data sanctioned by Finance. Trained Special Bid Associates to use tool. Increased sales and profits resulted.

BEFORE: SAP introduced with no training for product managers.
AFTER: While performing the Pricing **Analyst** role, I learned how to retrieve business critical data needed by product managers from SAP; created training document which became the basis for a two day class.

BEFORE: Multiple managers made conflicting decisions on the same product.
AFTER: As the Pricing **Analyst**, I chaired weekly meeting with all product managers so that plans could be discussed and coordinated. Confusion and rework were eliminated.

Business Planner | Financial **Analyst**

Nov 1995 – Dec 1998 • 3 yrs 2 mos

> Created unit, revenue, market share plan, interlocked with sales, reported actuals vs. plan.

> Improved factory forecast accuracy 29% through an analysis of all of the factors impacting unit sales.

Advisory Financial **Analyst**

Dec 1992 – Oct 1995 • 2 yrs 11 mos

> As an **analyst** I provided Financial and Business Planning support to US sales channel.

> Devised program enabling Sales Managers to customize budgets based on unique needs.

Sr. Pricing **Analyst**

May 1989 – Nov 1992 • 3 yrs 7 mos

> As an **analyst** I developed profitable, competitive pricing in response to special pricing requests. Reviewed proposed pricing with all levels of Sales, Product Management and Finance.

> Enabled Product and Channel Managers to sell their Data Networking products through three ordering systems by conducting training sessions.

Adding Keywords to the Skills Section

1. Go to your profile.

2. Click on 'Add profile section' and select 'Skills' as you see below.

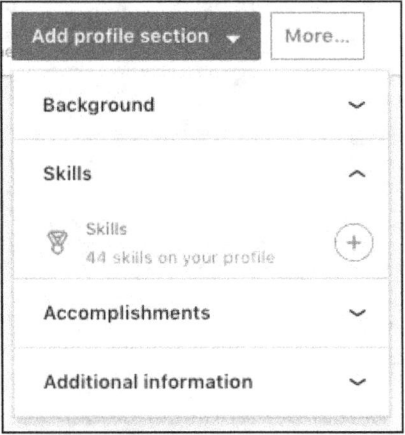

3. In the 'Skills' section, click 'Add a new skill.'

4. After clicking 'Add a new skill,' a dialog box like you see above will appear.

5. In the example below, I entered 'Analysis' to the right of the magnifying glass.

6. After clicking 'Add,' 'Analysis' appears at the end of the Industry Knowledge section.

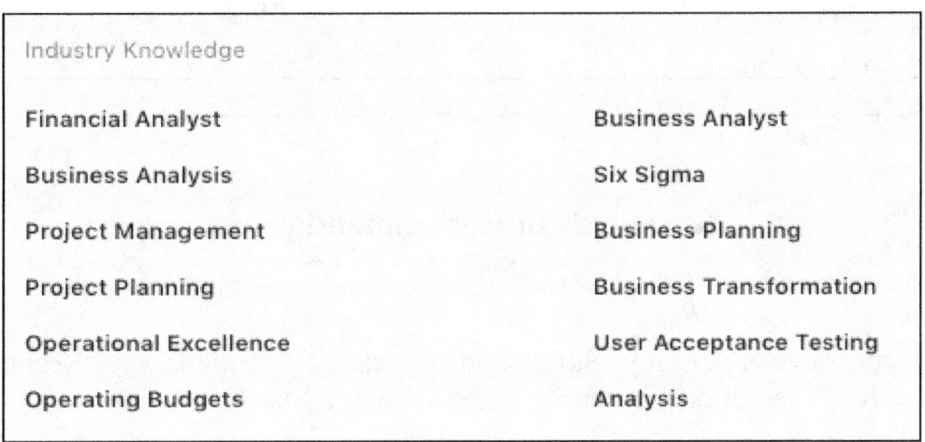

7. The two inserts below show the skills I added to my profile. As you can see, the term 'Analyst', appears nine times in my skills section. Besides 'Analyst,' I also added other skills which would be of interest to Recruiters and Hiring Managers.

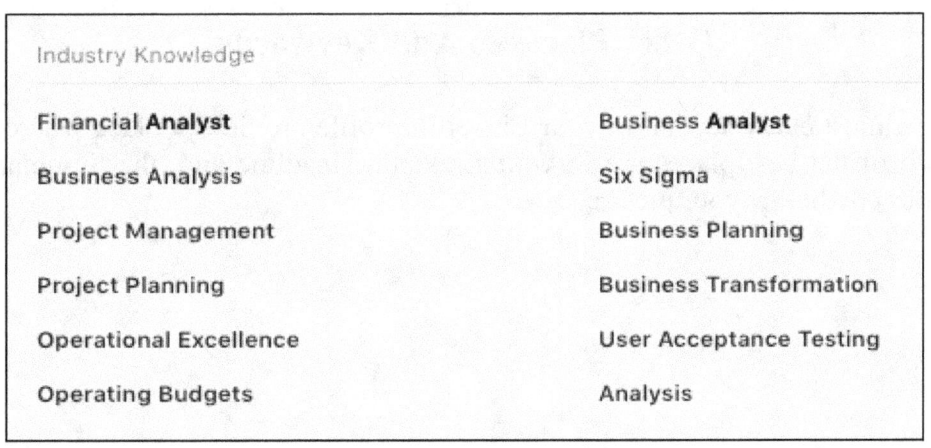

Conference Presentations	Training Seminars
Dynamic Speaker	Persuasive Speaker
Informative Speaking	Access Macros
Analyst	Reporting **Analyst**
Corporate **Analyst**	Planning **Analyst**
Budget **Analyst**	Product **Analyst**
Forecast **Analyst**	Business Operations
User Documentation	Responsiveness
Operational Execution	Analysis Reports
Analytic Reporting	

Keywords in Recommendations

Besides the keywords in my 'Skills' and 'Experience' sections, my 'Recommendations' also included seven (7) additional instances of the keyword, 'Analyst.'

There was no plan to make this happen; it just worked out that way. The best way for you to make it happen, is to ask those who recommend you to include your keyword in your recommendations. We'll talk about that more when we get to the 'recommendation' section.

Other Places to Add Keywords

While almost every section in your LinkedIn profile provides a place where you can add keywords, two of the best places are in your LinkedIn Headline and, the Summary portion of your profile directly below your picture.

Keywords Summary

As a result of these efforts, when I'm in my LinkedIn profile and click 'Edit' > Find and enter 'analyst,' 44 instances of 'analyst' were found in my profile.

analyst	1/44	∧ ∨

As you can see, if you're in my profile I did not follow the practice of 'stuffing' keywords into my profile.

Okay, I did that once and, someone reported me to LinkedIn, who then contacted me. So, I don't recommend that you do that! Anyway, that's the type of thing that will only make a recruiter mad.

By including all my roles and, making sure all my skills were listed, I got recruiters to call me.

Before you say, "It must be nice," keep in mind this was 2013 Florida. We started the year at 8% unemployment and, ended the year at 7% unemployment. There was a lot less opportunity than there is now.

The calls I got were for contractor roles. I initially resisted them, but ultimately said "yes" and, that was the best decision I made in this job search. Once I was employed, the unfortunate stigma of unemployment was removed, and I started getting interviews for full time positions.

What If I Don't Know the Keywords Recruiters Look For?

I attended Sunday school with a great guy, who's a lot like me, which is hard to find! One day, he told me he needed a new job as his former employer worked him so hard he wasn't seeing his family.

He had already quit, but he wasn't getting anywhere, so he asked if I could help. Here's what I showed him to do, to set himself apart from his competition using keywords.

Keywords attract Recruiters, however to identify the keywords for your skillset, you need to identify the various titles employers use for these roles.

Susan P. Joyce of www.job-hunt.org wrote an excellent post entitled, 'How to Identify Exactly the Right Keywords for Your LinkedIn Profile.'

In it, Susan shared how there can be multiple titles for the same type of work.

If this is your situation, go to Indeed.com/jobtrends and enter the different titles for your profession.

In Susan's example, the titles 'Social Networking Specialist', 'Social Media Specialist' and 'Social Networks Specialist' were entered into Indeed's Job Trends site.

I replicated the test and found, as Susan did, that 'Social Media Specialist' is the most popular title among employers, with 'Social Networks Specialist' being second. 'Social Networking Specialist' was not even in the running.

What If You Don't Know the Job Titles Corresponding to Your Skillset?

Even if you think you know all of the titles, it's a good idea to go through the following exercise. In Susan's example, 'social' was in all of the titles. In my friend's example, we believed 'wireless' would be in all titles. If you believe there may be a different title, you need to run that through the exercise below, as well.

I went to Indeed's website, entered 'wireless' and clicked 'Find jobs.'

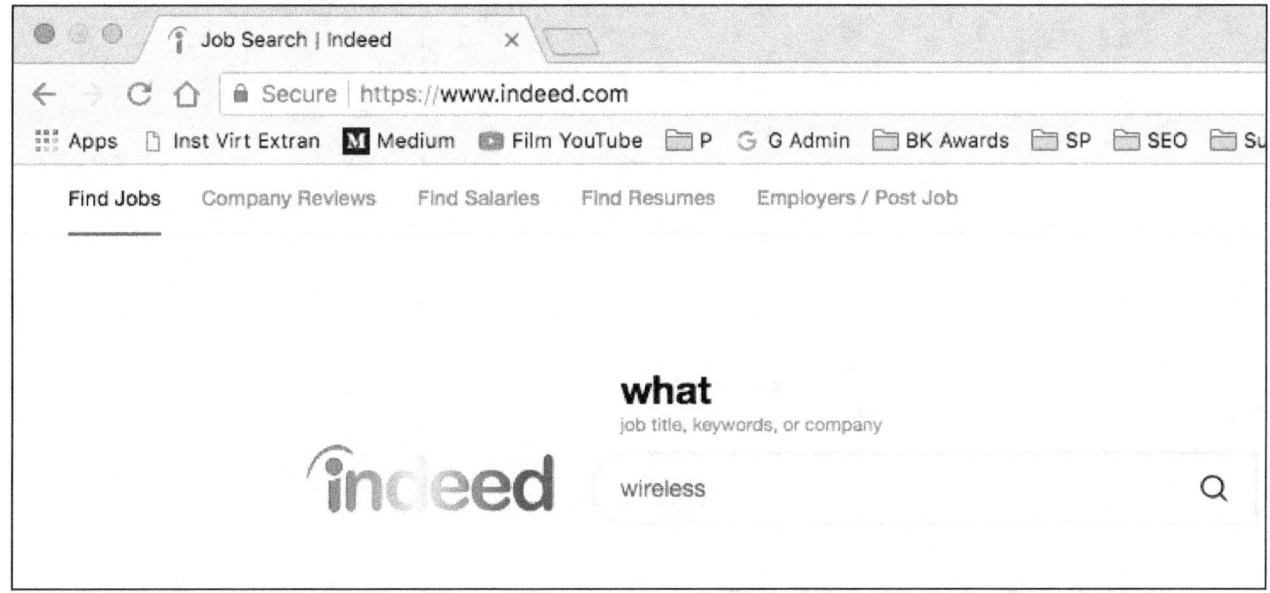

While reviewing these job descriptions, take time to read the description, to ensure it is a job in your field.

I realized early on using 'wireless' alone wasn't specific enough to hone in on only those jobs pertaining to my friend's field. I found 'WLAN' was frequently listed in those positions that were a good match for my friend. As a result, I added 'WLAN' to the 'wireless' search term.

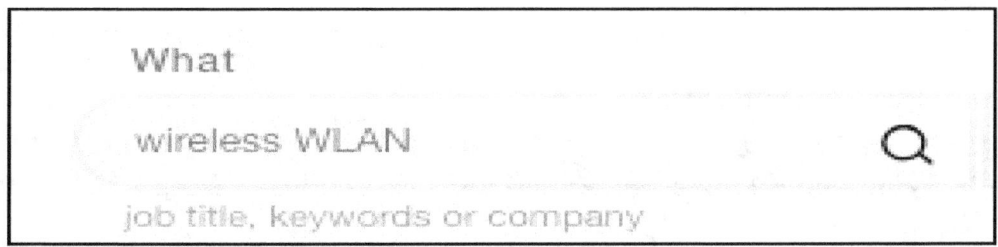

After clicking 'Find Jobs,' I added additional criteria to select those roles that were the best fit. I selected an '$85,000' Salary Estimate and 'Full-time' job.

Salary Estimate	
$70,000	(480)
$85,000	(415)
$100,000	(292)
$105,000	(251)
$120,000	(113)
Job Type	
Full-time	(557)
Contract	(46)
Internship	(10)
Temporary	(5)
Part-time	(2)
Commission	(1)

The following job titles were returned:

'Network Engineer;' 'Senior Network Engineer;' 'Senior Wireless Engineer;' 'Wireless Network Engineer;' 'Wireless Systems Engineer;' 'Systems Engineer;' 'Network Implementation Engineer.'

I then went to Indeed's Job Trends site: Indeed.com/jobtrends. While Indeed only populated data through July 2017, it's still valuable.

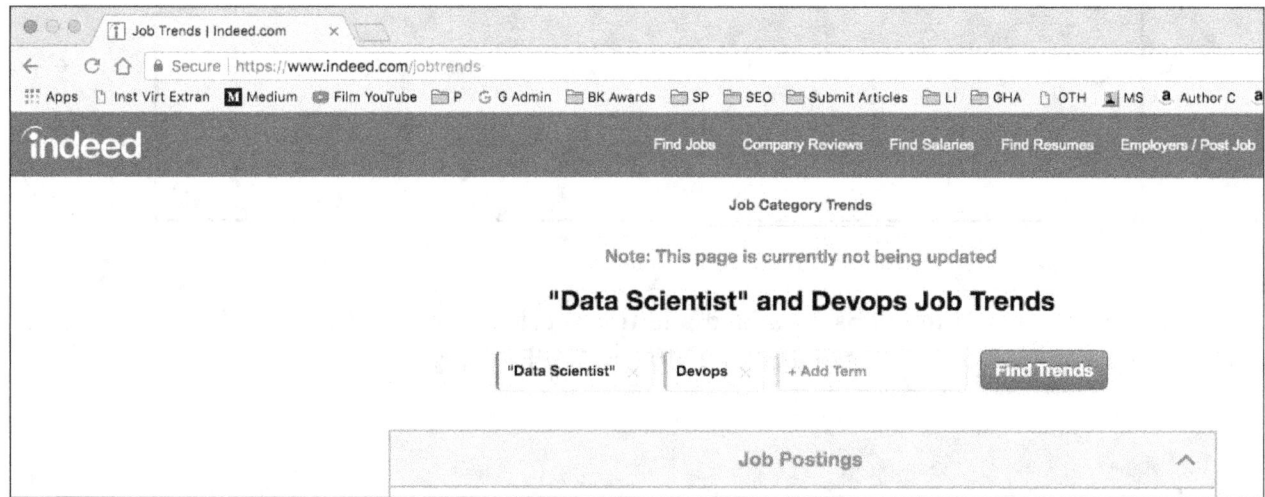

Next, I deleted the default titles you see above and entered the titles I had found. I also added versions with both 'Senior' and 'Sr.' in the title. I then clicked 'Find Trends.'

After clicking 'Find Trends' I selected a date in January 2017, because after that date the amount of information dropped significantly.

The chart revealed the most commonly occurring titles are 1.) 'Network Engineer;' 2.) 'Senior Network Engineer;' and 3.) 'Wireless Engineer.'

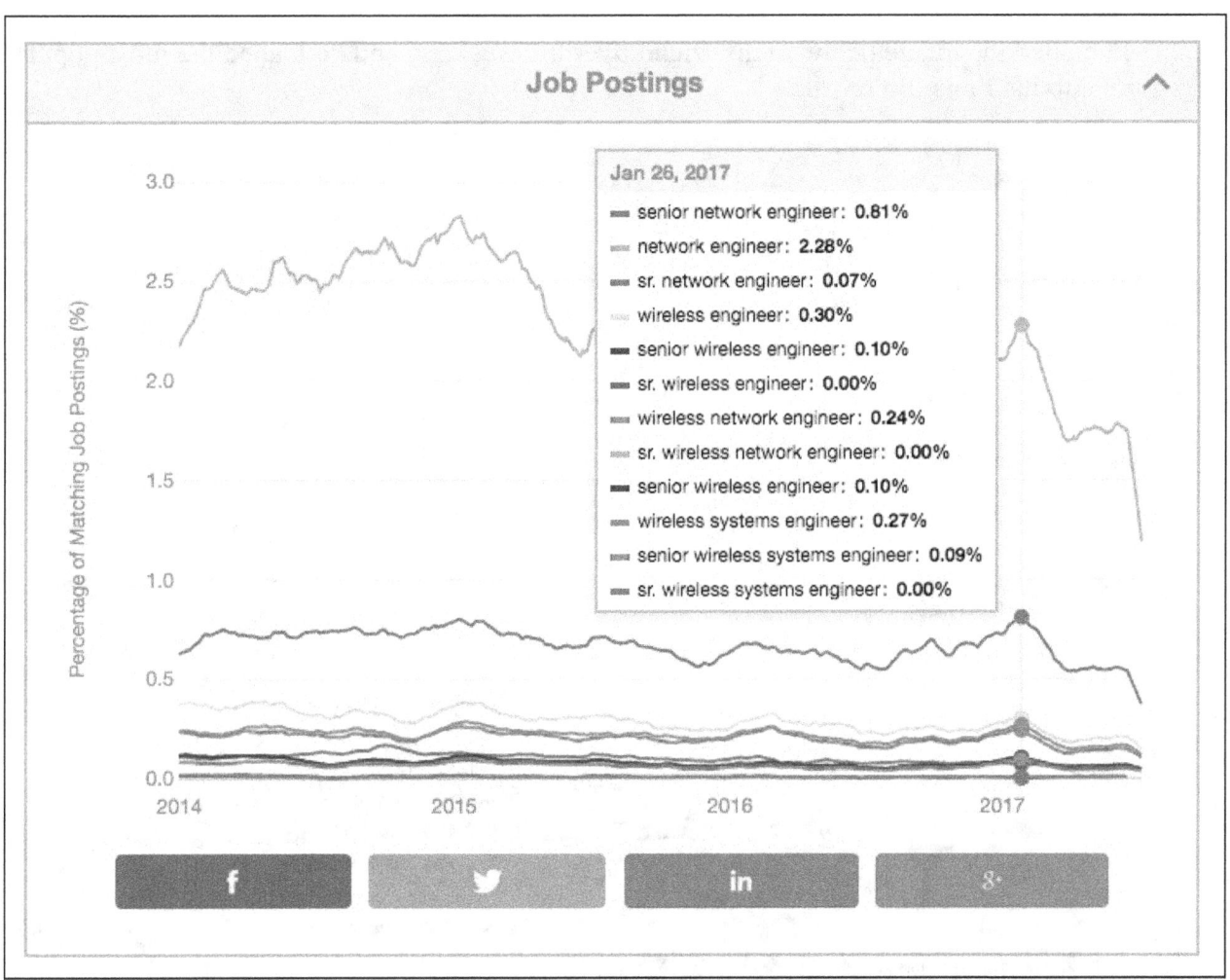

How to Find the Right Keywords

Once I identified the titles, I was able to move on and identify the keywords recruiters use to search for candidates with that skillset.

This entailed reading many job descriptions with the titles above. After reading through the job descriptions, I came up with several terms that were common across almost all of these jobs.

I then went back, to Indeed's Job Trends site - Indeed.com/jobtrends and loaded the keywords where I previously had loaded job titles. The insert below shows which terms appear most frequently in job descriptions.

I emailed the image below to my friend over the weekend and he loaded the most popular keywords into his LinkedIn profile.

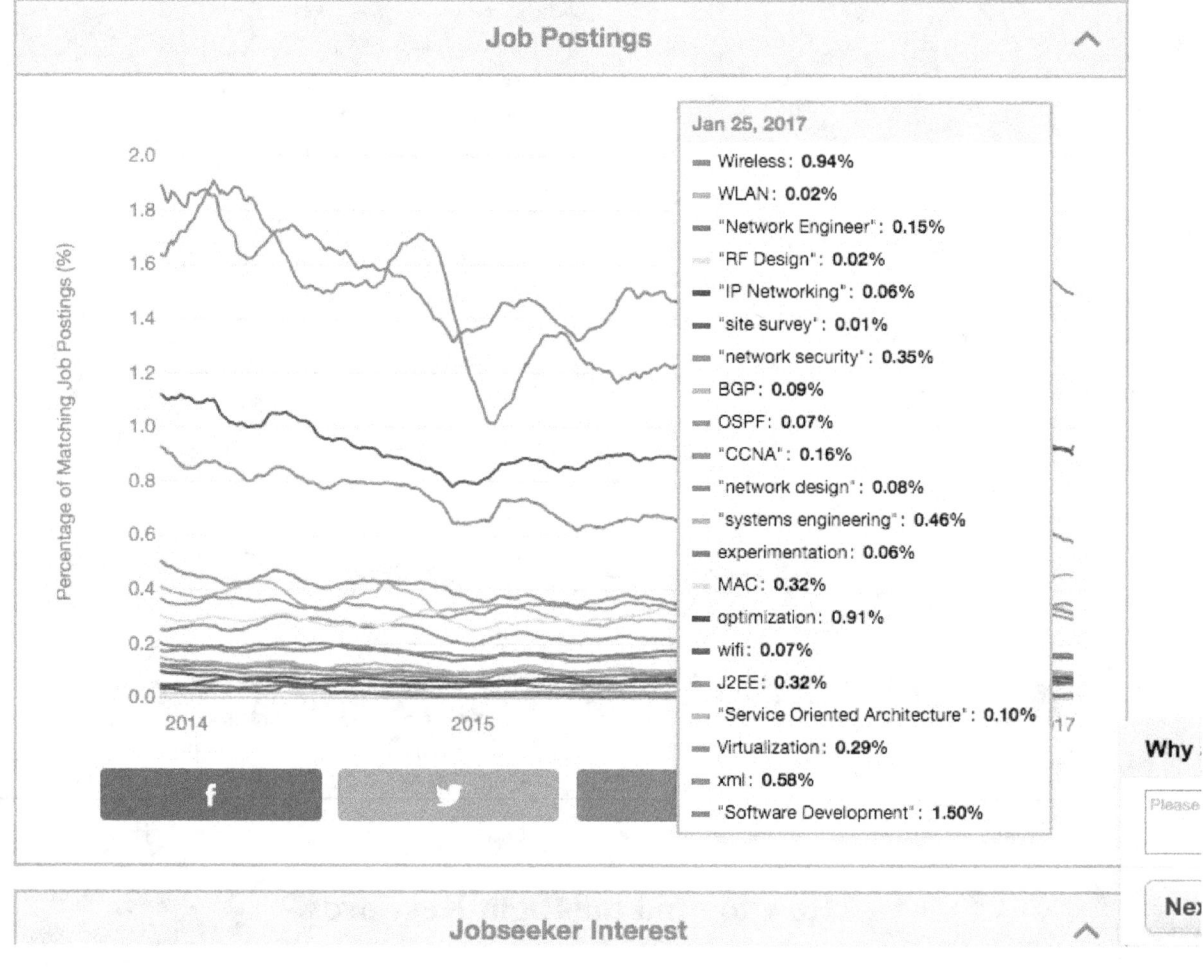

When I saw him the following Sunday he told me:

"Clark...I received several calls from recruiters, saying they saw my LinkedIn profile. This was the first time any recruiter ever mentioned my profile."

How to Kick the Competition off Your Profile

In case you didn't realize, when someone looks at your profile they also see your competition.

Go ahead, check out your profile! I say this because when I go to my profile there are 10 names next to it. (See insert below.)

Think about it. Here, you've gone to all that trouble of getting recruiters and hiring managers to find you. The last thing you want is a recruiter or hiring manager to be distracted by any of the 10 people listed under 'People Also Viewed.'

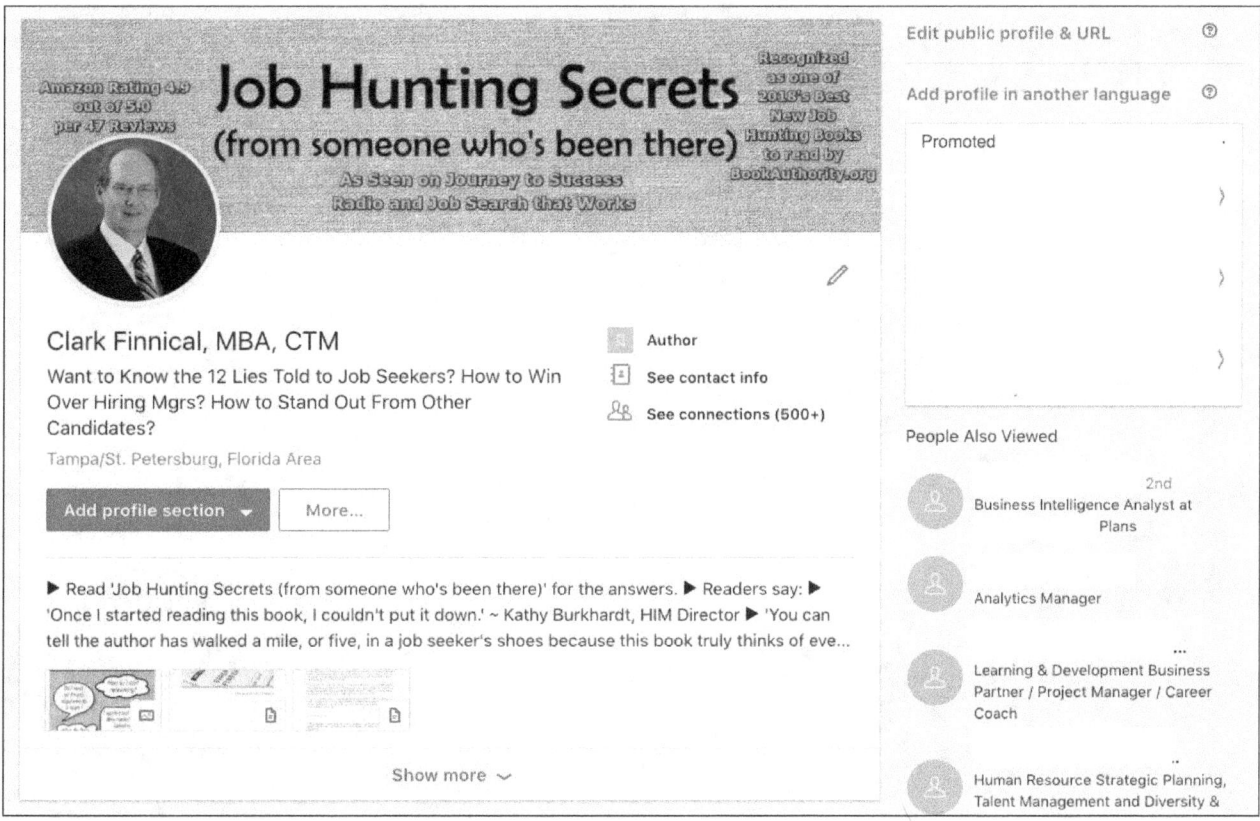

Fortunately, removing the competition is easy.

Click on the small round version of your profile photo where it says, 'Me' at the top of the LinkedIn site > Select 'Settings & Privacy.'

Select 'Privacy' > 'Viewers of this profile also viewed' > 'Change' > Select 'No' > Select 'Close' just like you see below.

Privacy	Ads

Viewers of this profile also viewed

Choose whether or not this feature appears when people view your profile

Should we display "Viewers of this profile also viewed" box on your Profile page?

No ⬤

Your Headshot, After Getting Found, Nothing Is More Important

According to Alex Todorov, an assistant professor of psychology at Princeton University:

"We decide very quickly whether a person possesses many of the traits we feel are important, such as likeability and competence, even though we have not exchanged a single word with them."

While we've always been told not to judge a book by its cover, Alex's studies show:

When we see a new face, our brains decide whether a person is attractive and trustworthy within a tenth of a second.

Alex and co-author Janine Willis conducted several experiments on approximately 200 people. In one experiment, they asked observers to look at 66 different faces, for 100 milliseconds, 500 milliseconds or one full second.

The experiments stemmed from earlier research conducted by Alex investigating the outcome of a political campaign.

In the earlier research, students found a direct correlation between how competent a campaigning politician's face was and how great his margin of victory in the final election. Alex said:

"We might assume that our judgments are founded on deliberate and rational thought processes, but observers had made their judgments about politicians based on a one-second look at their faces."

In a world where candidates are 'googled' before they are even considered for an interview, your LinkedIn photo has never been more important.

While many are familiar with Ladders' research revealing how recruiters spend only 6 seconds on every LinkedIn profile, a lesser-known fact is 19% of that time is spent on your LinkedIn photo.

Scary isn't it? However, there is no reason to be afraid because there is a tool that will enable you to select a picture that creates the right impression.

The tool is PhotoFeeler, their website is www.photofeeler.com

Does Your Headshot Help You or Hurt You?

I discovered PhotoFeeler while reading an article written by Christine Georghiou.[1]

I was intrigued by Christine's article, so I went to the PhotoFeeler site. I found I could easily upload my LinkedIn photo. There is also an option to upload your photo from Facebook or a photo on your PC or Mac.

Twenty people evaluated my photo. As you can see below, I was viewed as competent and influential, but when it came to likable, there was room for improvement!

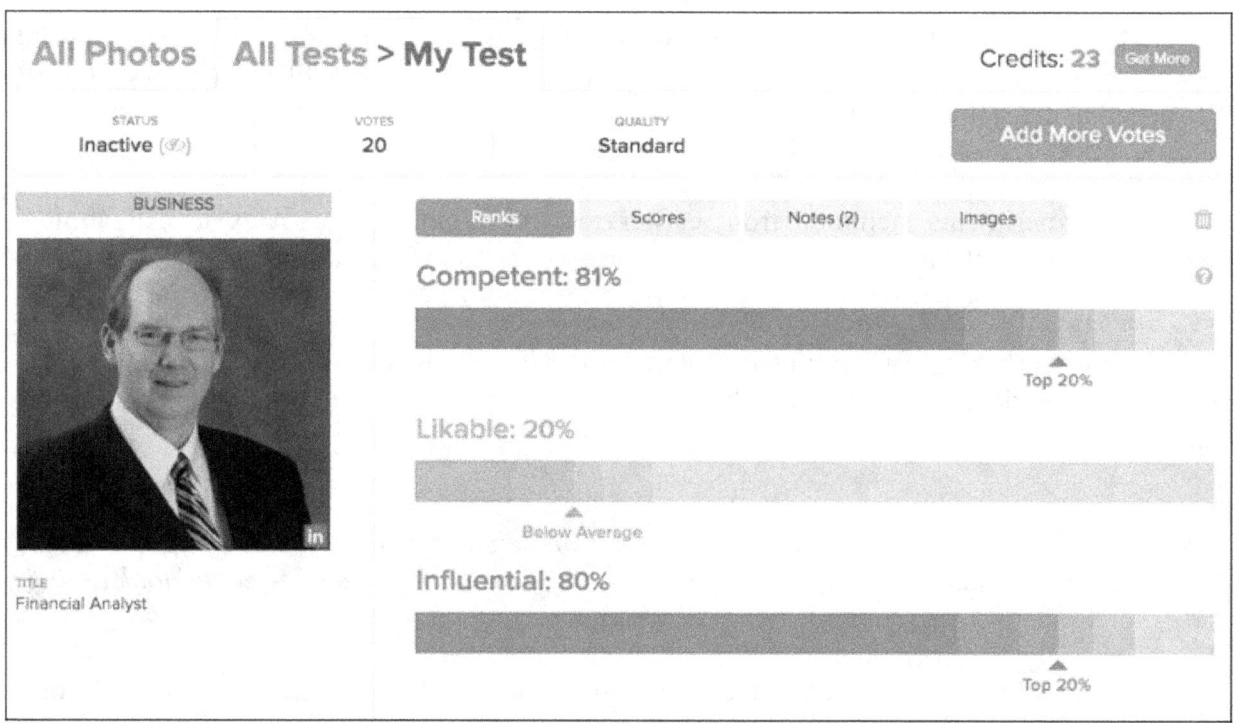

I was able to get the evaluation for free by evaluating photos from 20 other people. You can save time by purchasing reviews. I believe the first 50 reviews cost $7.00

When I tested my photo, I went to the bottom of their web page and 'Tweeted' about PhotoFeeler, while also sharing it on Facebook and LinkedIn. I believe this may have resulted in my photo being evaluated in less time.

How to Create the Best Possible LinkedIn Photo

In Christine's article, she also shares the following recommendations:

Smile, so your teeth are visible

- Research shows a closed mouth smile makes you appear half as likeable as someone who shows their teeth;
- Laughing while smiling increases likeability even more, however what you gain in likeability is offset by what you lose in competence and influence;
- Christine suggests spending a few minutes in front of the mirror so you can practice smiling before your photo is taken.

Always Squinch

- A squinch, or slight squint, increases the perception of competence and influence.

Emphasize Your Jawline

- When the outline of the jaw is visible all the way around, studies have shown it increases influence, likeability, and competence scores.

Dress Appropriately

- Studies found formal dress increased perceived competence and influence scores more than all other tested factors; For example, men in a light-colored button-down shirt with a dark suit jacket and tie scored higher than those dressed in bright or trendy outfits.

Look at the Camera

- Tests show the more people look at each other, the more they like each other. This is also true when looking at a photo of someone;
- When sunglasses or hair block people's eyes, even from a glare or a shadow, their photos get lower ratings than people who looked at the camera.

Head and shoulders, or head to waist shots are best

- It turns out face-only close-ups bring likeability scores down and, full body photos negatively impacted competence and influence.

Avoid photos that are too dark or saturated with color

- Photos that are too dark or have high color saturation brought scores down. Experts recommend putting yourself in front of light, filtering in through a window or posing in a lamp-lit room, to give your photo a warm glow.

Consider a bright background color

- While she couldn't offer a clear set of guidelines for choosing colors for your profile picture, Christine suggested testing alternative ways of making your profile photo stand out with a bright background color. Of course, testing like this usually takes a professional photographer or a Photoshop expert, but it's worth considering.

Still Uncertain About PhotoFeeler?

If you're still not sold on PhotoFeeler, read these posts on it:

The Muse: https://www.themuse.com/advice/what-does-your-linkedin-photo-say-about-you

The Avid Careerist: http://www.avidcareerist.com/2015/03/15/profile-photo-research-infographic/

The American Genius: https://theamericangenius.com/social-media/evaluate-profile-picture-photofeeler/

What Do You Have to Say for Yourself? Your Headline

OK - You've been found! You've chosen a stellar headshot - PhotoFeeler ranked you in the top 90% for Competency, Likeability & Influence!

Getting found is the first step.

Choosing a photo that communicates the right qualities is second.

Now that you have their attention, how are you going to use your headline?

Are you actually going to squander all of your hard-earned attention with a headline that says, "Looking" like 52,340 people?

Are you really going to throw away all of that effort with a headline that says, "Unemployed" like 238,851 other people?

I'm not trying to be cruel. I'm trying to remind you of the opportunity before you.

You're on stage - you've got their attention! You need to continue the sales process so your phone rings. Consider these four job seekers:

Which of These Four Headlines Will Lead to Interviews?

John Smith
Looking

Terry Johnson
Laid Off

Jane Smith
PMP-certified project manager. Known for successfully leading multi-million dollar projects in developing countries.

Tom Johnson
Customer-focused pro who can program every robot in your factory. Specializing in ABB, FANUC and Kawasaki robots.

If you said, Jane's and Tom's, you're right![1]

Jane and Tom realize:

- They've got less than 6 seconds to get a recruiter or hiring manager's attention;[2]
- They realize, after the photo, the LinkedIn headline may be the only part of their profile that a Recruiter or hiring manager looks at;[3]
- Their LinkedIn profile is the first place most people will look when they apply for a new job;[4]
- LinkedIn is the place where recruiters and headhunters are most likely to come across your profile.[5]

Jane and Tom understand:

- Recruiters think a candidate is desperate if they have headlines like John and Terry;[6]
- Recruiters perceive that candidates are sitting back and waiting to be found if they have headlines like John's & Terry's;[7]
- Recruiters are always touting the strengths of their candidates to prospective employers. Hence, it only follows that Recruiters would expect job seekers to be touting their strengths as well;[8]
- Recruiters believe candidates undermine their value when they use headlines, like John and Terry's.[9]

How to Create a Strong Headline

While your headline defaults to your current job, title and, employer, it's easy to change.

Go to your LinkedIn Profile > Click on the 'blue pencil' on the far right of the top of your profile.

You can now edit.

Your top priority should now be crafting a headline that maximizes your value and helps you to be found.

How to Create Headlines That Maximize Your Value

Jenny Foss shows us how good a headline can be in the link below. In fact, the two winning headlines at the beginning of the post are from Jenny's Forbes post: How To Make Your LinkedIn Headline Stand Out.

Jenny's expertise in creating LinkedIn headlines stems from the fact that she is a busy Recruiter.

As a result, when she scans hundreds of profiles, she asks:

"Why should I read your profile?"

She expects the job seeker's headline to answer that question.

Per Jenny, the best LinkedIn headlines include these listed elements:

- Succinctly showcase your expertise, your value, or you're 'so what.'

Jenny provided this headline example:

PMP-certified project manager – Known for successfully leading multi-million dollar projects in developing countries.

- Speak to your target audience and speak in terms of their interests.

Per Jenny, the headline below does just that:

Customer-focused pro who can program every robot in your manufacturing facility. Specializing in ABB, FANUC, and Kawasaki robots.

Liz Ryan, the founder of the Human Workplace, says:

"Your headline is critical, because it tells us how you see yourself."

Liz tells the story of a job seeker who is not like every other job seeker. She works in a particular way. She wrote this LinkedIn headline:

Office Manager/Business Air-Traffic Controller ISO Stressed-Out CEO to Make Sane

Liz shared that this job seeker wants everyone to know how she does her job. She compares it to air-traffic control. She loves helping crazed CEOs organize their day and their projects. Liz said the minute after the job seeker updated her headline she got calls from recruiters![10]

Pete Leibman, author of the book, I Got My Dream Job and So Can You, offers a 4-step process to create successful LinkedIn headlines:

Say WHAT you are.

Say WHO you help.

Say HOW you make their life/work better.

Give PROOF that you are credible.

Pete offers these headline examples:

Executive Recruiter and High-Performance Coach who helps you create a stronger career. Featured on Fox/CBS/CNN. (This is Pete's own LinkedIn headline.)

Fundraising consultant who helps major non-profits raise more money. Clients include the Red Cross and YMCA.

Personal Trainer who helps high school athletes get stronger and faster. Certified by the American Council on Exercise.

Pete stresses each of these headlines immediately communicate what the person does, who they help, how they help them, and their credibility.[11]

Your Headline Can Help You Get Found

Because the words in your headline are more highly weighted in LinkedIn's search algorithm, strive to include the keywords recruiters use to search for candidates with your skills.

Will Your LinkedIn Summary Pass The 6 Second Test?

Remember, you're building a path for the Recruiter or Hiring Manager.

Getting found is the first step.

Choosing a photo that communicates the right qualities is second.

Selecting a headline that explains why they should read your profile is third.

Before they read through your experience, they'll read your summary.

Will your summary have the right stuff?

Recruiters spend about 6 seconds on their initial 'fit/no fit' decision.

Because you have no guarantee anyone will read below your Summary, it must send the right message! The Summary I used when I was a job seeker is found below:

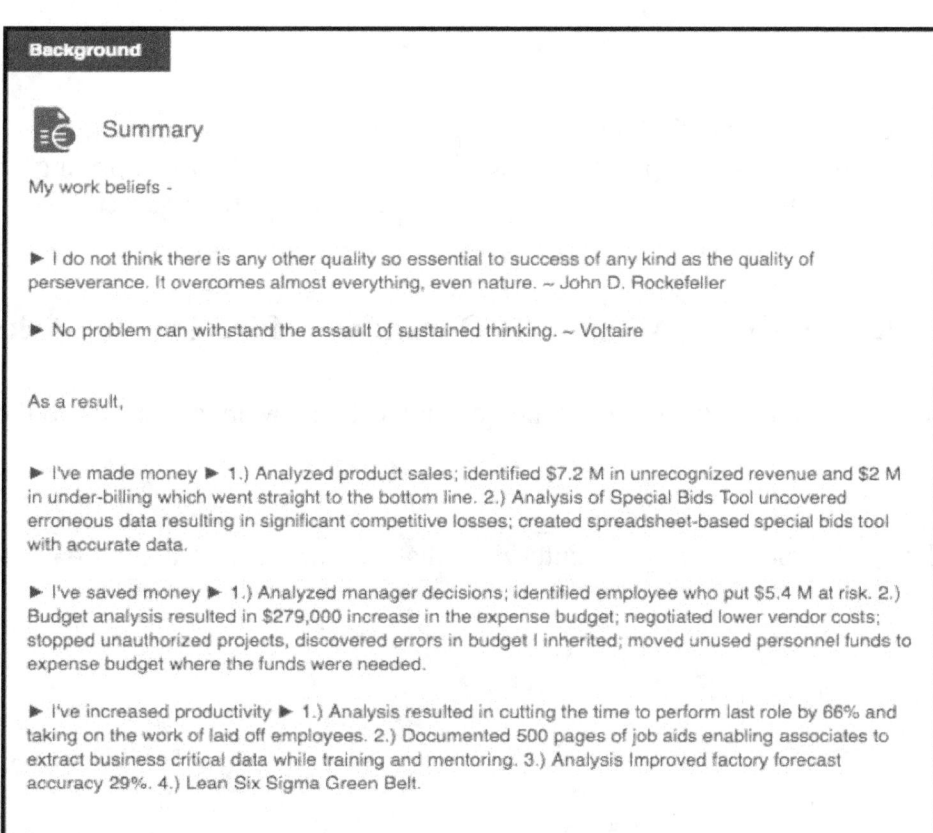

53

Work Beliefs

As you can see in the first insert above, I started my summary with two quotes that communicate my belief in the power of persistence and, sustained thinking to overcome problems. Whenever I'm asked, "Tell me about yourself," I share these quotes.

Answer the Hiring Manager's Questions before They're Asked

I created a summary that answered the questions Hiring Managers bring to the interview.

As described in my book, Job Hunting Secrets (from someone who's been there), once the Hiring Manager decides during the interview that you are in fact a candidate, she wants to know:

Have you made money?

Have you saved money?

Have you increased productivity?

Have you made a difference?

There is no reason to wait to tell these stories. Once you tell these stories, you'll stand out from all the other candidates. Since you've gotten their attention, take advantage of the opportunity.

Former Manager's Testimonials

Because few people understand an individual better than someone who's managed them AND, few people's opinions matter more to Hiring Managers, I included quotes from two former managers that show my strengths, savings and how I made a difference.

Strengths Finder's Strengths Assessment

Because Gallup's Strengths Finder Assessment is one of the best, if not *the* best strengths assessment out there, I attached a copy of my assessment to my profile. (See my LinkedIn profile to read the Assessment.) In addition, I also included three quotes from my assessment.

After rereading my Strengths Finder results, if I was in the job market again, I'd use these quotes instead

Per Gallup's Strength Finder,

I see patterns where others see complexity.

I have a constant need for achievement.

I take psychological ownership of anything I commit to.

If you haven't taken the assessment you can purchase it here: StrengthsFinder 2.0

After buying the book, which was $14.99 as of August 2018, you will need to pay for your assessment results. I did mine a few years ago. I just paid for the top five themes report versus the larger 34 theme report. At the time, that was between $50.00 and $75.00

This is a worthwhile investment because it helps you better understand yourself. At the same time, the assessment is also something that will be of interest to any Hiring Manager or future Supervisor.

Here's some additional background on Strengths Finder:

- As of August 2018, Strengths Finder 2.0 is the 90th best-selling book on Amazon.
- In addition, more than 2400 people have been trained by Gallup to use the Strengths Finder assessment, to help clients fully realize all their unique strengths.

Work Examples

When I was in the job market, I attached examples of my work. (Just ensure that no proprietary information from past employers is included in those attachments.)

Closing on Your LinkedIn Summary

Because everyone's experiences are different, I strongly encourage you to create a LinkedIn Summary which describes:

- How you've made a difference in prior positions;
- Awards you've received and, why you received them;
- Obstacles you've overcome;
- Outstanding Achievements.

No matter what you put in your LinkedIn summary, it should demonstrate how you are different from other candidates.

If you're Still Asking Why You Should Go to All of This Effort…

It's because the Recruiter hasn't called you yet! You haven't landed that job yet! You need them to be wowed by your summary so that they'll continue reading and, go to your experience section.

Does Your Experience Section Generate Interviews?

In case you forgot, you're building a path, so the Recruiter or Hiring Manager discovers why you're the right choice for them.

You've taken the correct steps to get found.

You've chosen a photo that communicates the right qualities.

You've selected a headline that explains why they should read your profile.

You've also written a summary with just the right amount of information to make them want to read more.

You've got them reading this far!

Your work experience expands on everything in your summary.

Now is your time to share all those achievements and, accomplishments where you've made money, saved money, improved productivity and, made a positive difference.

Put yourself in the Hiring Manager's shoes.

She wants to know how *you* made a difference.

She needs to know why she should give *you* the time of day.

Are you just like everyone else or, are you going to make her look good?

Your Experience Section & Your Achievement Stories

Your achievement stories play an essential role in your resume, LinkedIn profile and, in your interview.

If you haven't read Job Hunting Secrets (from someone who's been there) you may not be familiar with achievement stories.

Each achievement story contains:
- The situation you were in;
- The obstacles you faced;

- The actions you took;
- The results of your actions.

These are also known as S.O.A.R. statements. Another name sometimes used is S.T.A.R. statements.

I dedicate 16 pages of Job Hunting Secrets (from someone who's been there) to the creation of achievement stories. Hence, if you're not familiar with these, I strongly recommend purchasing the book.

Your achievement stories explain how you are different. These stories contain the accomplishments in your resume, as well as the longer stories that make up the experience section of your LinkedIn profile.

I took time to count the number of words in the work experience part of my resume and, the number of words in the experience section of my LinkedIn profile.

As you can see in the insert below, the experience section of my LinkedIn profile has almost twice as many words as the work experience part of my resume.

	Number of words from my achievement stories
My resume work experience	466
My LinkedIn experience section	826
Actual interview	The only limit is the time available for the interview

That's because in very rare exceptions, a resume is expected to be no more than one or two pages. The experience section of your LinkedIn profile is only limited by the number of achievement stories you decide to share.

In the first insert below, you can see how I used the 'Greater Than' symbol also known as an 'Angle bracket'[1] as bullets to separate my achievements.

Operations Analyst | Program Manager | Financial Analyst

Apr 2011 – Dec 2012 • 1 yr 9 mos

> Reduced time to perform Operations Manager role by 66%; after analysis showed tasks could be batched and performed at the end of the month. Asked Director if I could take on the responsibilities of laid off employees.

> Increased open rates 100% after analysis of Business 2 Business mailer process and researching best practices.

> Budget analysis resulted in $279,000 increase in the expense budget; negotiated lower vendor costs; stopped unauthorized projects, discovered errors in budget I inherited; moved unused personnel funds to expense budget where the funds were needed.

> Maximized impact of Marketing department through on-going analysis of current and planned spending. Ensured Marketing associates used 99-100% of their budget every quarter.

> Project managed implementation of Client Choice Award, resulting in 600 employees receiving customer nominations for exemplary service ensuring its future success.

In the insert below, I describe my achievements in a way which emphasizes the positive impact I had while working there. In addition, I've quantified my achievements wherever possible.

Business Analyst | Financial Analyst | Business Operations

Oct 2002 – Oct 2010 • 8 yrs 1 mo

BEFORE: Offer Creation process flawed.
AFTER: Analysis revealed misconfigured offers; worked with other departments to correct errors. Recognized $7.2M. Implemented process to prevent future errors.

BEFORE: Offer Discontinuance Approval process broken.
AFTER: Analysis revealed manager discontinued active offers generating $5.4M annually. Created reporting enabling product managers to see financial impact of their decisions.

BEFORE: Analysis identified 5000 under-billed Maintenance customers. Existing processes flawed.
AFTER: Worked with others through an analysis of the problem resulting in developing systematic solutions. $2M generated as 5000 customers' billing corrected; Billing failure rate cut by 50%; Two internal audit items and corresponding IT projects successfully driven to closure.

BEFORE: Ending Services Support on legacy products very time consuming.
AFTER: Analysis of the process and teaming with another SME resulting in a time-based project management tool enabling managers to know what to do, when to do it and who to work with.

BEFORE: Expertise to generate business critical data limited to small number of Associates.
AFTER: As a Business Analyst, I created 500+ pages of job aids enabling others to retrieve business critical data. Documentation analysis ensured that even novices could quickly get up to speed.

The inserts below speak to other facets of my role that are not reflected in the accomplishments above.

Lean | Kaizen | Six Sigma Specialist

Jan 2007 – Sep 2010 • 3 yrs 9 mos

> Supported Director in Kaizen through ongoing research and analysis; he said, "Your help was invaluable to this team in terms of the questions you helped answer and the policy documents you helped develop and shared."

> Received Ovation Award for my role in the Six Sigma project which resulted in improvements in the SKU implementation process.

> Supported Senior Manager in the Customer for Life Six Sigma project which made the first significant steps to document the ending services support process.

Project Manager | Analyst

Jan 2006 – Aug 2010 • 4 yrs 8 mos

> > Development / delivery of training for Indian Offer Management Team. Delivered materials a week ahead of schedule.

> > Cross-departmental team responsible for resolving under-billing of 5000 customers.

> > Three audit-driven corporate IT initiatives from an analysis and writing of the business requirements to User Acceptance Testing and implementation.

The first position below addresses a role I volunteered for while working as a Business Analyst.

The second position, below it, follows the strategy used above, which clearly demonstrates the difference I made in that role.

Reporting Analyst

Oct 2002 – Jul 2010 • 7 yrs 10 mos

> Created quarterly Global Maintenance Operations Review for executive consumption; Analysis identified key revenue, margin and business performance metrics that will be of interest to Leadership.

> Product managers could not tell if their portfolio's were successful; analysis of a Finance-sanctioned report determined that it could be used to produce monthly portfolio revenue reporting.

> Provided business-critical data as needed to support management decision-making; on-going analysis enabled me to act as a consultant to Leadership who could explain the "so what" of the business-critical data.

Pricing Analyst | Operations Analyst

Jan 1999 – Oct 2002 • 3 yrs 10 mos

BEFORE: We were losing a large number of deals and did not know why.
AFTER: Analysis of Special Bids tool identified erroneous cost data. Created Special Bids tool with accurate cost data sanctioned by Finance. Trained Special Bid Associates to use tool. Increased sales and profits resulted.

BEFORE: SAP introduced with no training for product managers.
AFTER: While performing the Pricing Analyst role, I learned how to retrieve business critical data needed by product managers from SAP; created training document which became the basis for a two day class.

BEFORE: Multiple managers made conflicting decisions on the same product.
AFTER: As the Pricing Analyst, I chaired weekly meeting with all product managers so that plans could be discussed and coordinated. Confusion and rework were eliminated.

Don't Believe You Have Any Achievements?

First, don't sell yourself short by comparing your achievements to my achievements. I'm 59 years old. I've had a few years to make achievements.

I go over collecting and quantifying achievements in my book, Job Hunting Secrets (from someone who's been there). Some of the best places to find your achievements are:

- Performance reviews;
- Awards;
- Promotions;
- Managers and coworkers;
- Emails;

- LinkedIn recommendations.

I also recommend asking yourself these questions:
- What problems did you solve?
- How do you work differently from your coworkers?
- How did you change your department?[2]

Your Earliest Positions

As you can see below, I included valuable details. At the same time, I combined positions for the simple reason that older positions are less likely to be of interest to Hiring Managers. While there are fewer details, I continued to share key accomplishments. Wherever possible, I also shared quantified accomplishments.

Business Planner | Financial Analyst

Nov 1995 – Dec 1998 • 3 yrs 2 mos

> Created unit, revenue, market share plan, interlocked with sales, reported actuals vs. plan.

> Improved factory forecast accuracy 29% through an analysis of all of the factors impacting unit sales.

Advisory Financial Analyst

Dec 1992 – Oct 1995 • 2 yrs 11 mos

> As an analyst I provided Financial and Business Planning support to US sales channel.

> Devised program enabling Sales Managers to customize budgets based on unique needs.

Sr. Pricing Analyst

May 1989 – Nov 1992 • 3 yrs 7 mos

> As an analyst I developed profitable, competitive pricing in response to special pricing requests. Reviewed proposed pricing with all levels of Sales, Product Management and Finance.

> Enabled Product and Channel Managers to sell their Data Networking products through three ordering systems by conducting training sessions.

LinkedIn Recommendations <u>Can</u> Lead to Your Dream Job

If a Hiring Manager was told she could only have one piece of information about you, practically every Hiring Manager would choose a well-written recommendation from your former supervisor.

Why?

Because that person supervised you and, that person knows everything the Hiring Manager who is considering hiring you would like to know.

That person knows your strengths and weaknesses.

That person is also less likely to stretch the truth as her reputation is on the line.

Four Ways Hiring Managers' Recommendations Can Advance Your Career

1. It can be placed at the beginning of your cover letter, so it stands out and gets the attention of the busy Hiring Manager, HR Manager or Recruiter;

2. It can win over anyone reading your LinkedIn recommendations;

3. It can be used within your LinkedIn experience section to demonstrate how you made a difference;

4. It can be shared in your interview to demonstrate your value as an employee.

When I interviewed five years ago for my current role, my cover letter looked like this:

Dear ▓▓▓▓▓▓

I am very interested in the Financial Analyst - ▓▓▓▓▓▓▓▓ opportunity (Job Number: C▓▓▓▓▓▓).
My qualifications match your needs very closely and can make an immediate impact for you.

Consider these quotes from past Leaders -

➤ Director ▓▓▓▓ said, *"I am constantly impressed by his thoroughness. No detail goes past him without him asking if it makes sense or could be better - this particular skill of Clark's has saved our team a lot of money."*

➤ Sr. Manager ▓▓▓▓ said, *"His exceptional analytic skills have helped deliver a long line of business improvements and successful projects."*

➤ District Manager ▓▓▓▓ said, *"He possesses an outstanding ability to articulate ideas and decision alternatives. In critical situations, this formed the basis for necessary business consensus building around his proposals."*

Each italicized quote came from a LinkedIn recommendation written by a former boss.

The bosses who wrote these recommendations understood how important recommendations can be in someone's career.

Because these individuals had also been Hiring Managers, they understood what Hiring Managers look for when considering candidates for an open position.

What Hiring Managers look for in an interview is addressed in the 'Hiring Manager's Secrets' chapter of my first book, Job Hunting Secrets (from someone who's been there).

During the interview, the Hiring Manager's first priority is to determine whether you are truly a candidate for the position. They do that by getting to know you, so they can answer the following questions for themselves:

1.) Can you do the job?

2.) Will you like the job enough to stay there?

3.) Can we stand to work with you?

If the Hiring Manager determines that you are in fact a candidate, the next question in their mind is, 'How do you compare to all of the other candidates?'

The candidates that stand out communicate:

1.) How *they* made money;

2.) How *they* saved money;

3.) How *they* increased productivity;

4.) How *they* made a difference.

It's rare for a candidate to have all four of these qualities. At the same time, if you don't have one of the first three qualities, it is imperative that you show how you either made a difference at past employers, or at least how you are different from other candidates. Well-written recommendations can do this for you.

Hiring Managers are going to care more about what your former bosses put in their recommendations. That's not to say your peers' recommendations won't be valuable. It is to say, Hiring Managers know that few people know you better than the people you worked for.

In addition, Hiring Managers also know our former bosses are usually at a higher level than our peers and, therefore are less likely to stretch the truth. For not only are you being judged, but they are being judged by what they have written.

How Do I Get A Great Recommendation from My Boss?

First, don't confuse recommendations with references.

Historically, references played a critical role when moving from one position to another. While references are still important and, still needed, LinkedIn recommendations can do more than references ever did.

Hiring Managers have to request references from you and, then call that person. With LinkedIn recommendations no calls are required. Job seekers preparing for the next interview should always strive to have detailed recommendations on their LinkedIn profile, from both former and current bosses, as well as peers they've worked closely with.

Recommendation Strategies

My Old Recommendation Strategy

In the past, when I sent a recommendation request, it looked like this:

Dear ____,

I would greatly appreciate it, if you would recommend me.

If I am out of work in the future, the words in your recommendation could determine whether I get interviews and therefore whether I get hired again.

I've read the most effective recommendations are based on your personal experience and, call out the individual's strengths.

Here are some qualities you may want to include in the recommendation -

Versatility, analytical skill, process orientation, project management, business planning, creative problem solving, thoroughness, continuous improvement, mastery of complex issues, initiative, strong communication skills, perseverance and innovation.

Thank you,

Clark

Where My Old Recommendation Strategy Fell Short

Between 2006 and 2016, I sent 130 recommendation requests to bosses, peers and other leaders at my employers. I received 54 recommendations.

13 of the recommendations were excellent. 5 were from bosses. 2 were other members of upper management I had worked with. 6 were from peers who I had worked closely with.

32 of them I would describe as good.

4 were 'OK.'

5 were not posted because they were not well-written or did not send a strong message.

I'm glad that I asked my bosses, as I shared their recommendations with Hiring Managers in interviews. I included them in cover letters and, put a few in my LinkedIn summary.

Here's a recommendation that was never posted:

"I found Clark to have the following qualities when we worked together: versatility, analytical skill, process orientation, project management, business planning, creative problem solving, thoroughness, continuous improvement, mastery of complex issues, initiative, strong communication skills, perseverance and innovation".

When I looked at the verbiage I received, it made me wonder if a change in strategy might be needed. You think?

My New Recommendation Strategy

While I will continue asking for recommendations from current bosses, former bosses, members of upper management and, peers I had worked with, going forward I will follow the advice Jessica Smith, aka the Resume Butterfly, provided in her excellent post, 'How to Give — and Get — LinkedIn Recommendations.'[1]

Specifically, I will include a draft recommendation which the recommender can either use as is, edit or, if they prefer, write their own.

A draft recommendation can be particularly helpful if it has been a while since you worked for your boss. Because, whatever you can do to help your former boss remember, what you did will help them write a stronger recommendation for you.

Here's an example:

A former boss asked me to create a report that had never been created before. If I were to ask her for a recommendation, here is what it would look like:

Hi ____,

I would greatly appreciate it, if you would recommend me.

Given your busy schedule, I provided a draft recommendation, which you can use as is, edit or write your own.

When Clark worked for me, I asked him to create a report measuring the financial impact of the Stop-Loss. No one had ever done this before. When we discussed his progress, I always gave him an easy out if he felt it could not be done, but he never took me up on my offers.

He worked closely with a subject matter expert on the topic. The report took time, as there was a lot to understand. In the end, Clark produced exactly what the CFO and I were looking for. We never understood the financial impact of the Stop-Loss and now we do. As a result, we can now make wiser, more informed decisions.

I was impressed by what I saw in Clark. He did not care that others had not succeeded before him. In fact, he seemed to revel in the challenge. He likes taking the effort to understand complex things. As a result, what was once a problem is no longer a problem.

Perhaps, what impressed me most about Clark was his perseverance. It did not matter that it was taking a long time. He persisted and ultimately succeeded.

Given my experience with Clark, I believe he would be a valuable addition to any team.

If I am out of work in the future, the words in your recommendation could determine whether I get interviews and therefore whether I get hired again.

Thank you,

Clark

While the new strategy will be more time-consuming, it will result in better recommendations.

Keep this in mind as you request recommendations in the future, since it is highly likely recommenders will use much, if not all your draft recommendation. Strive to create draft recommendations that are different from each other, otherwise, your recommendations may start to look too similar, which can shed doubt on their authenticity and value.

The Power of a Boss's Recommendation

To reinforce my earlier point, a boss's recommendation is one of the most powerful things you can put in front of a Hiring Manager.

Hiring Managers are in a difficult position. Unless someone has referred you, they know next to nothing about you.

Boss's recommendations are valuable because:

They give Hiring Managers insight into what they can expect if they hire you;

No one knows what an employee can do better than, a former manager.

A manager will only write what she is certain about. After all, her reputation is on the line. She will not say person X is great when person X is not great.

Avoid Posting Weak Recommendations

No matter what you might think, it is exceedingly rare that anyone will know you did not post their recommendation. If they write a recommendation, they assume you posted it.

It is much better to never display a poorly written recommendation, than to post it and make the person who is reading your profile, question your wisdom and decision-making ability.

Consider this, if a poorly written recommendation appears as the first recommendation in your profile, do you think others will continue to read your profile to look for a good recommendation? No! They'll go on to the next candidate.

Using Recommendations in Cover Letters

I have no doubt that you will encounter folks who will tell you "Recommendations have no place in a cover letter."

If this was 1980, I would agree with them, but it's not! The internet changed everything. You're lucky to get anyone's attention! So, if you can include strong recommendations at the beginning of your cover letter, you will stand out. That's how people get hired and that is all that matters.

How to Request A Recommendation Within LinkedIn

LinkedIn is always improving, so it's possible that the process will be different. At the time of writing, this is the process:

1.) Go to the profile of the person who you're going to ask to recommend you. (You need to be connected to this person, that is, you need to be a first-degree connection.) You will know you're a first-degree connection, if you see '1st' to the right of their name, as you see below. If you're not connected, you'll need to send them a connection request;

2.) Click the 'More...' tab directly below the picture and, name of your connection;

3.) After clicking 'More...', click 'Request a Recommendation,' as you see below;

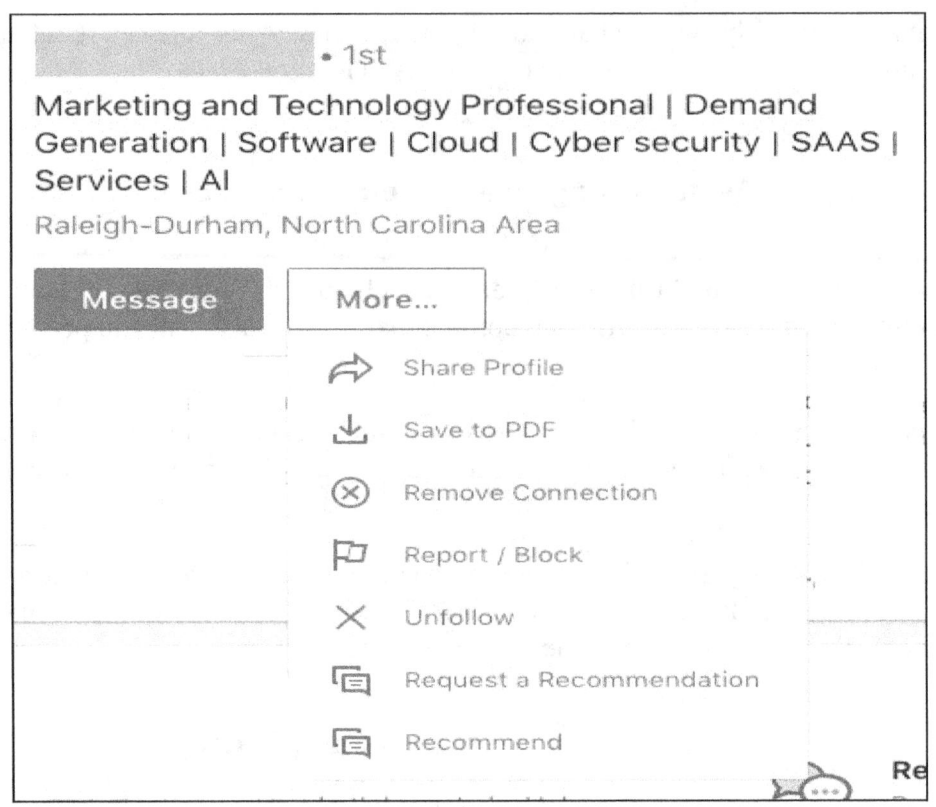

4.) After clicking 'Request a Recommendation,' the window below appears. In the insert below, I went to a former supervisor's LinkedIn profile. After requesting the recommendation, I was prompted to select how I knew the person. I selected 'Managed you directly' and then I selected my position at the time.

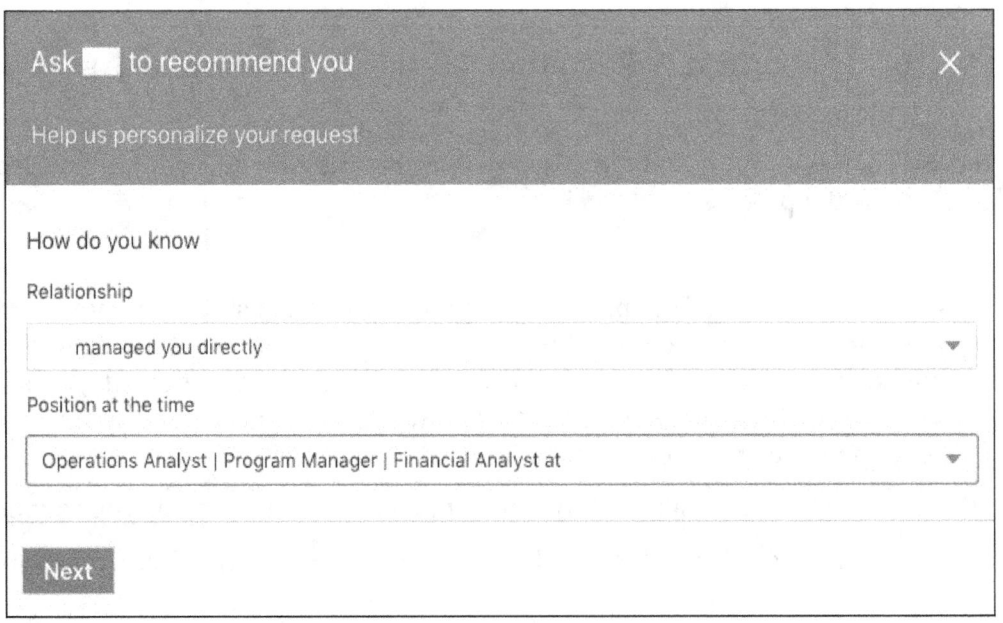

5.) After clicking 'Next,' you will see the dialog box below;

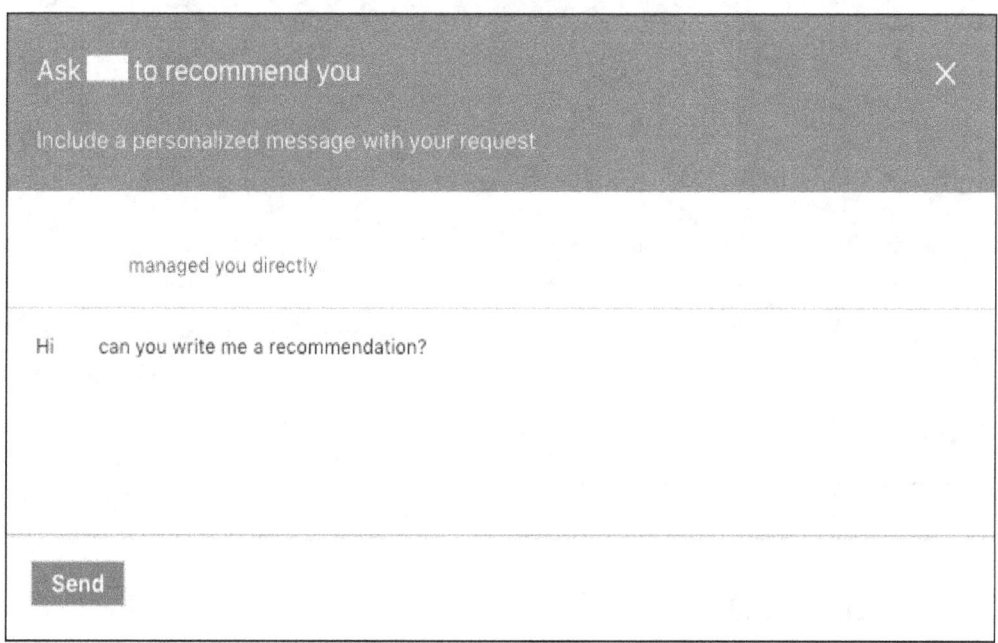

6.) At this point, you can leave the default message that you see above, or you can edit the message, as I did. As you can see below, I deleted the default message and copied the recommendation request that you saw above.

7.) Next, click 'send.'

8.) Because, not everyone goes on LinkedIn regularly, I strongly recommend calmly and gently reaching out, ideally by phone, but if that is not possible then by email or text so they realize you've asked for their help. This is a time when you want to invest as much as possible in this relationship by speaking with them, and then explaining the reason for your call.

If you want to know the best way to ask for a recommendation on your iPhone, Android or any other device within LinkedIn, click on your small round profile picture near the top of the page which has 'Me' underneath it. Select 'Help Center.' A search bar will appear. Enter, 'How to request a recommendation.' That will give you everything you need for your device.

Endorsements or Recommendations?

If you're wondering why I haven't spoken more about endorsements, consider my experience below:

When endorsements were introduced, I began receiving a tremendous number of messages from connections who I had never worked with, who live in countries I've never visited.

Each message said:

I've endorsed all your skills, please endorse my skills.

When I explained I only endorse people who I've worked with, some of them got mad.

I finally adjusted my endorsement settings, so no one could endorse me. (See instructions below.)

I could not understand why these people put so much value on endorsements!

MJS Executive Search of Scarsdale, NY, penned an article entitled:

"The Truth about LinkedIn Endorsements."

Here are some excerpts from that article:

"What does a LinkedIn endorsement really say about you? Nothing."

"All an endorsement says is that you have a friend nice enough to recognize your functional knowledge of a particular area. If you truly feel that strongly about someone, take the time to write them a recommendation. It is a lot more genuine than clicking the endorsement button."[2]

Aline Lerner posted an article on the interviewing.io blog entitled:

"LinkedIn endorsements are dumb."

The slogan of this blog is 'better interviewing through data.' Aline shared:

"We were curious about whether we could actually come up with some numbers that showed how useless endorsements can be and, we weren't disappointed."

Aline compared endorsements to interview performance. She found no relationship between how heavily endorsed someone is and their technical ability.

Aline also looked at whether having any endorsements mattered with regard to interview performance. Her analysis found having any endorsements at all, or none whatsoever, had no impact on their interview performance.

It is for these reasons Aline said:

"LinkedIn endorsements are just noisy crowdsourced tagging."[3]

Joseph Liu, a career consultant and, host of the Career Relaunch podcast shared:

"In the context of a hiring decision, I've never encountered a situation where endorsements made one bit of tangible difference."

Joseph said, "Endorsements are not objective; are not necessarily credible; and tell me nothing about quality."[4]

It is, for all these reasons, that I recommend you focus on getting great recommendations and forget about endorsements.

Adjusting Your Endorsement Settings

Go to your 'Skills' section and click the 'pencil' to the right of 'Add a new skill.'

Click the 'Adjust endorsement settings' link at the bottom of the window.

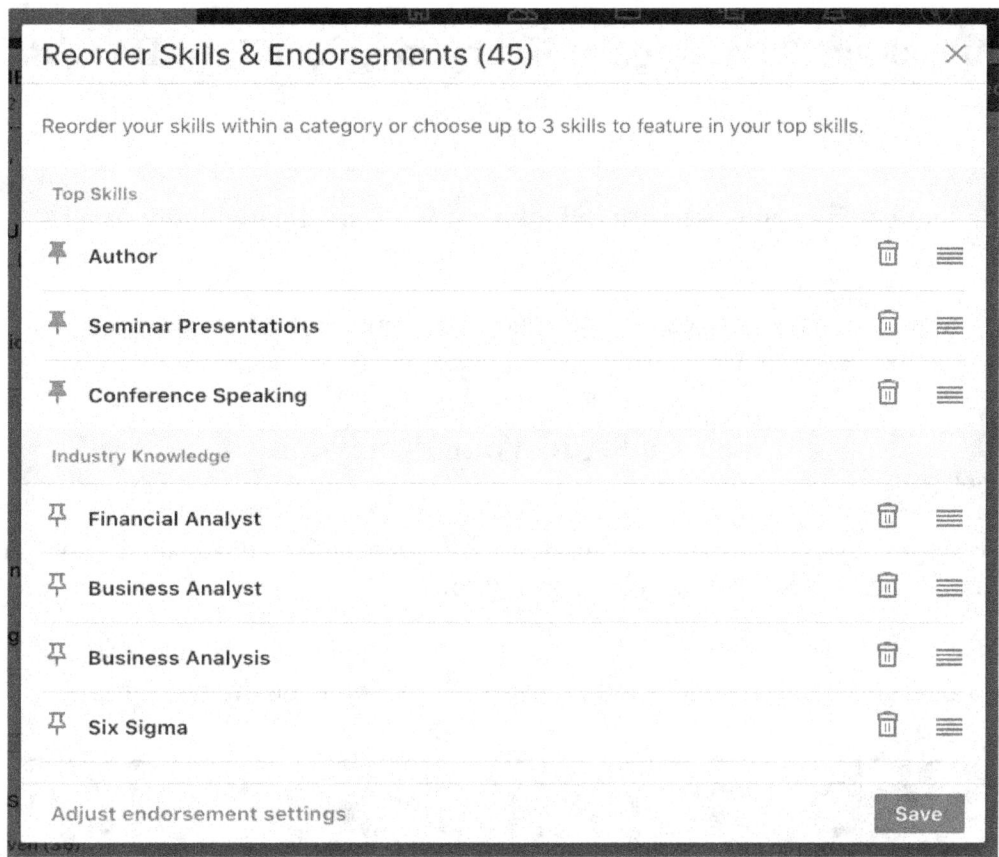

When the next window opens, there will be a toggle switch to the right of 'I want to be endorsed.' Click the toggle to the left so you see 'No' as you can see below.

Are You Taking Advantage of Everything You Can Do with Your Name?

You might be scratching your head, thinking, "What can I do with my name?"

In LinkedIn you have options and, 40 spaces to exercise those options.

You Can Add Your Profession

Scott Singer says adding your profession after your name will make "…your credentials pop off the list," when a Recruiter searches for that role.[1]

To do this, go to your profile. Click the 'pencil,' which is on the far right.

After clicking the pencil, you will see the following:

Now you can easily enter your title, as I've done below.

After clicking 'Save,' it looks like this:

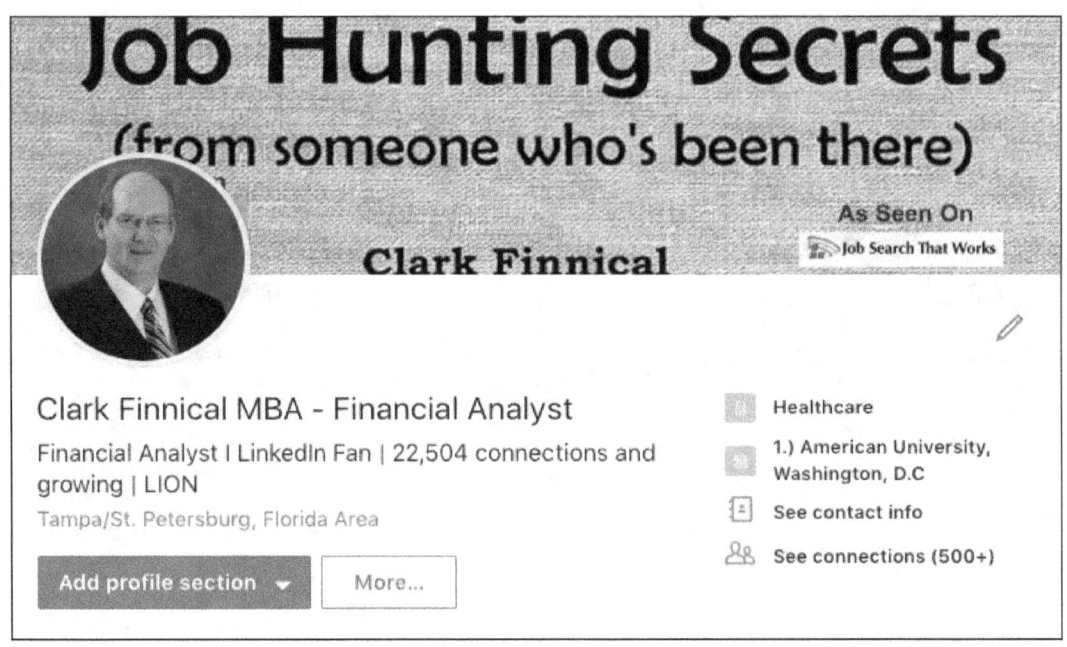

You Can Add Your Professional Credentials

Nicola Fairweather recommends adding your professional credentials after your name.[2]

By following the same steps outlined above, here's how my name looks when I add my MBA, Lean Six Sigma Green Belt and Competent Toastmaster certification.

You worked for these credentials, let the world know it!

You Can Add Former Names

Not everyone may know you by your current name. Thankfully, LinkedIn makes it easy to add former names. On your profile page, click the 'pencil.'

Click on 'Add former name.' You can choose to make your former name visible to only your connections (1st level connections), only your network (1st, 2nd and 3rd level connections) or to all LinkedIn members.

To illustrate what LinkedIn can do, I entered my wife's name and, maiden name as you can see below.

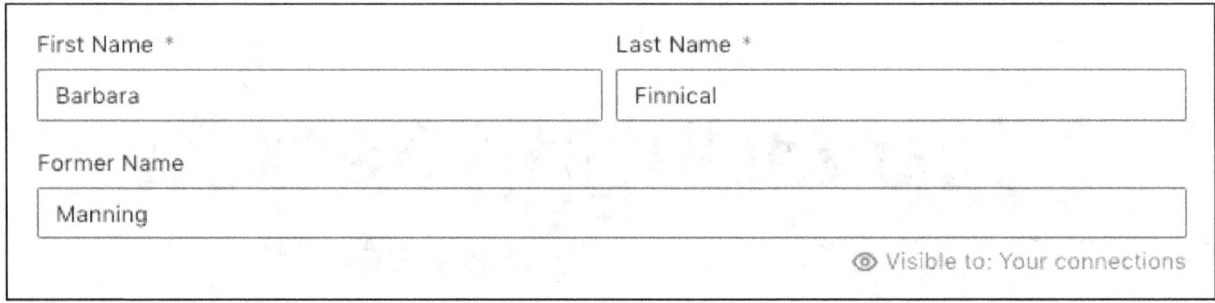

After clicking 'Save,' Barbara's name appears on the profile, like you see here.

Barbara (Manning) Finnical

You Can Add Your Nickname

Some of us aren't known by our actual name. If I entered 'Skip' in the 'Former Name' field it would look like this:

Is Your Public Profile turned off?

Make sure your public profile is turned on, so Recruiters and Hiring Managers can see your full name. Do this by going to the upper right part of your LinkedIn profile and, clicking 'Edit your public profile.'

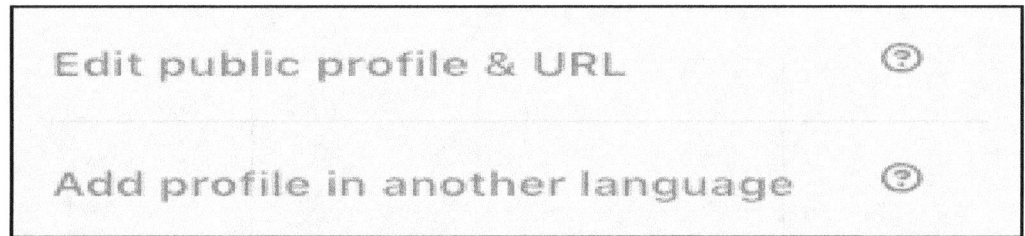

After clicking 'Edit your public profile,' your public profile appears. As a job seeker or anyone who is open to being contacted by recruiters, you want to ensure your profile's public visibility is set to 'On' as you see here.

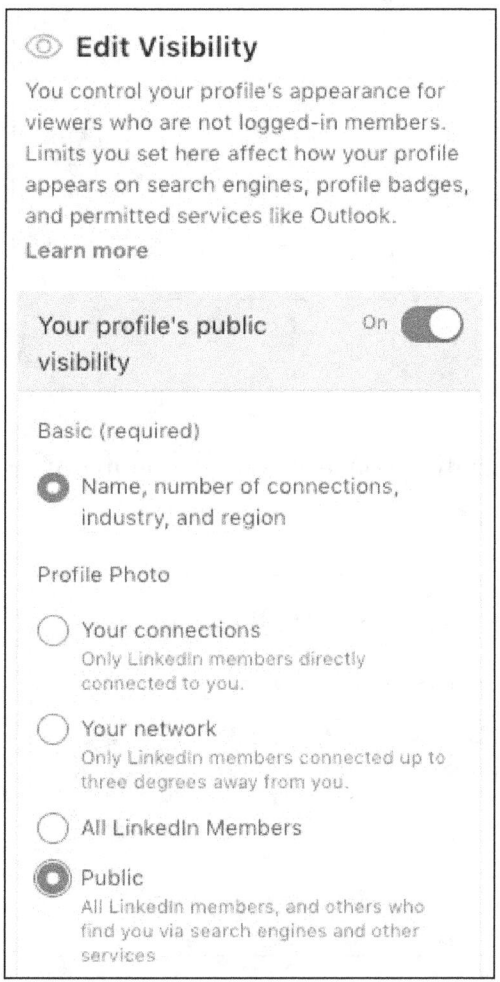

Everyone's needs are different, hence LinkedIn lets you choose who can see your profile photo, as you can see in the above insert.

In addition, LinkedIn lets you control which sections of your profile are visible to others. Of course, anyone who is interested in landing a job or a better job is best served by making all sections visible.

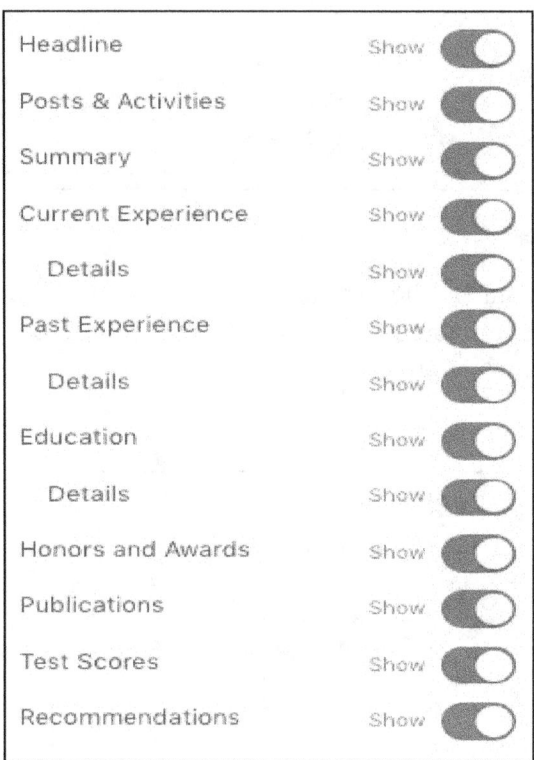

As you edit your public profile, you also have the option of making your profile available in other languages.

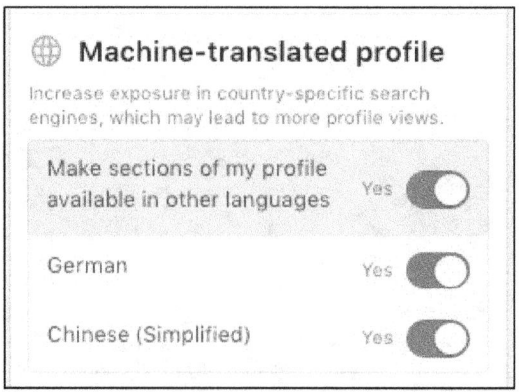

Another option which I haven't taken advantage of yet is creating a 'Public Profile badge.' After clicking the 'Create a badge' button, you are provided with code, which can be used on your blog, online resume, or website.

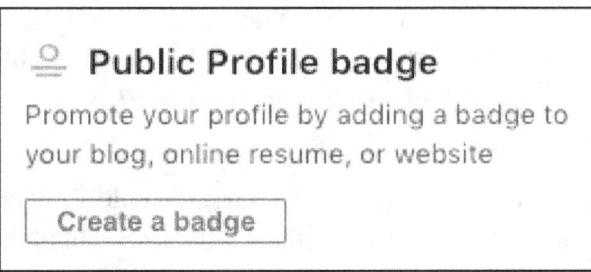

How and Why You Should Update Your Public Profile URL

While you're editing your public profile, create a personalized URL. Do this by clicking the 'Edit URL' link which is found on the top right of the 'Public profile settings page.'

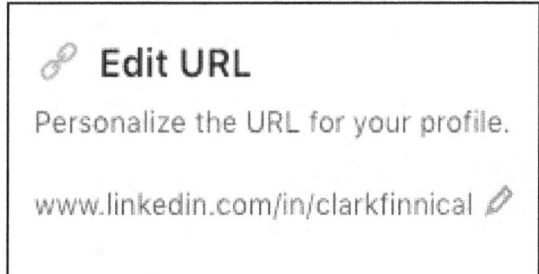

When you click the 'pencil,' the box will appear like you see below. I've already modified my URL.

Why did I personalize my URL and why do I recommend that you do the same?

A personalized URL is more pleasing to the eye than the original URL, which contains numbers, dashes and, sometimes letters.

It also makes it easier for people to recognize the URL is yours. In the original URL that LinkedIn provides, it's harder to find your name.

When personalizing your URL, you may need to add your area code or zip to your URL, if someone has already used your name.

Misspellings

Since many people have names like mine that are frequently misspelled, it is wise to enter the possible misspellings somewhere in your profile. That way, if someone is looking for you, but doesn't know how to spell your name, they can still find you.

Some people suggest doing this in the summary. I don't want to take away from my summary, so I put the misspellings at the end of the education chapter below. See the upcoming section for more information.

Is Your Education Section Helping or Hurting?

My education section is inserted below.

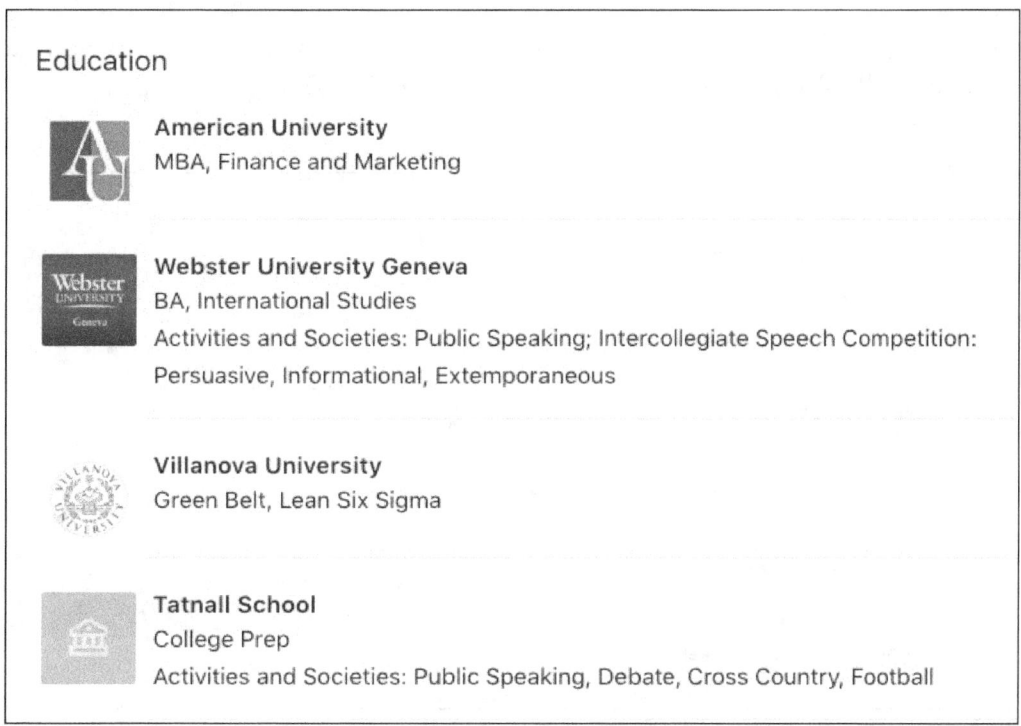

One of the nice things about LinkedIn is you can add college or university icons to your profile. Adding these icons makes your profile more interesting and therefore helps to draw attention to your profile.

Here's how to do it:

If you've added the name and haven't chosen one of the pre-populated schools, your school will look like this, as mine once did. Click on the pencil on the far right.

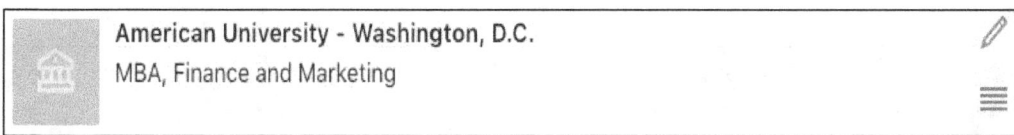

After clicking, you will see the window below:

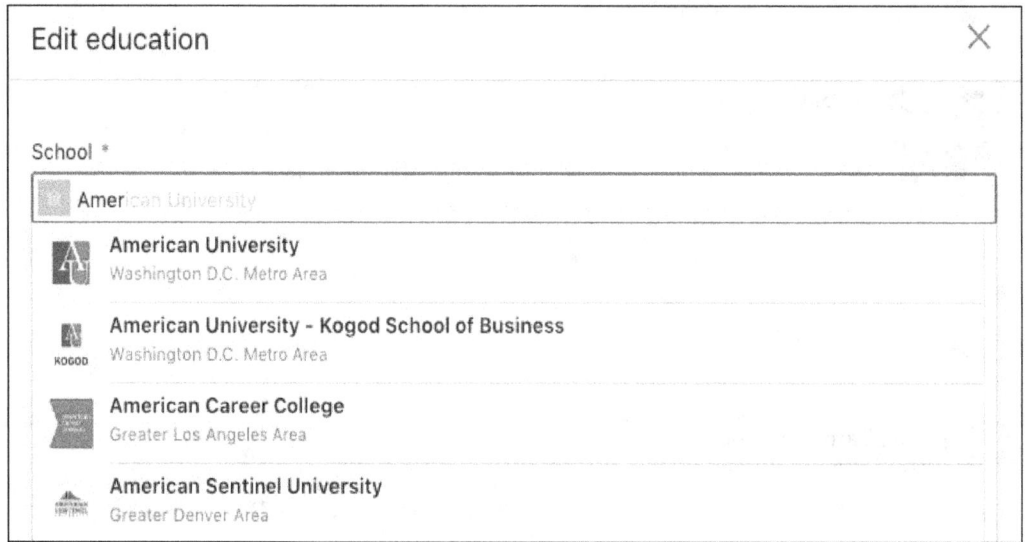

Delete what you've typed in. Then start to type the first few letters of your school. As you can see below, all of the schools that begin with those first few letters appear.

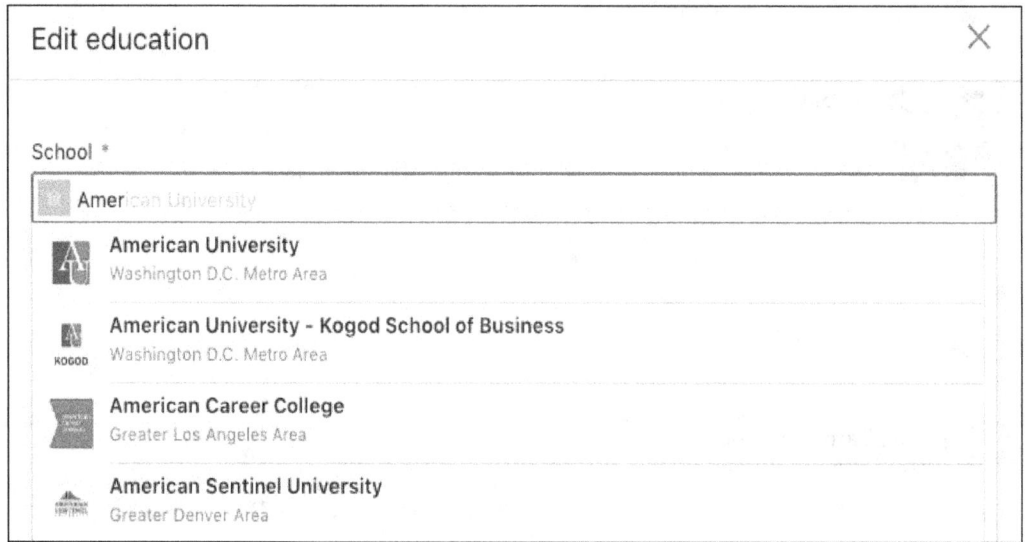

Next, I selected my school and clicked 'Save.' As a result, my graduate school which previously looked like this...

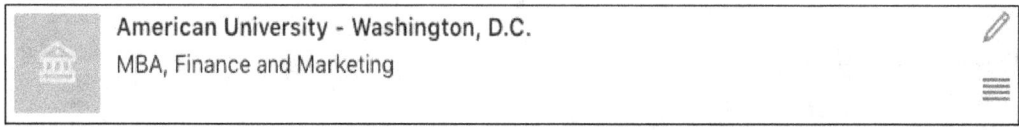

Now looks like this...

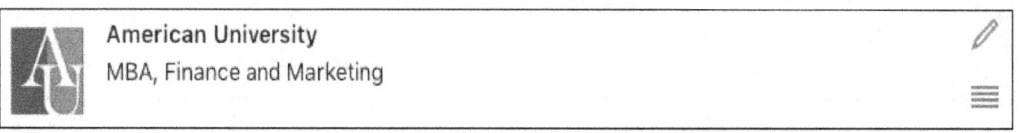

In addition, the icon for the first school in your Education section appears to the right of your headline at the top of your profile.

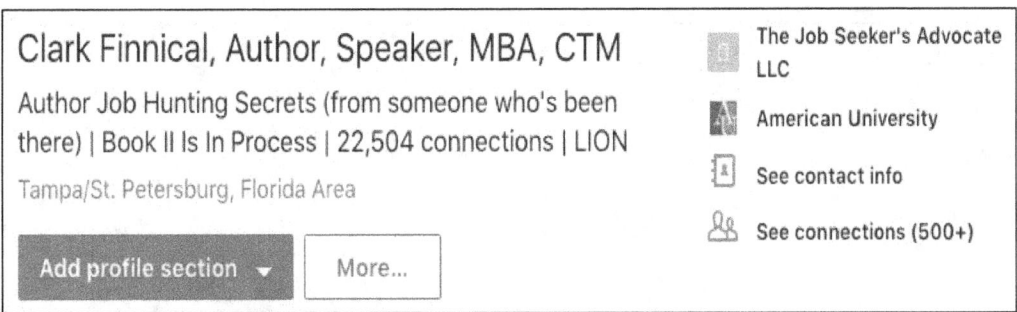

Putting Your Most Important Education First...

One of the nice features of the Education section, and almost all the LinkedIn profile sections, is the ability to move the most important parts to the top.

LinkedIn's default setting lists the most recent education first, but sometimes that doesn't serve our best interests.

For example, my Green Belt below is the most recent education I have attained, however with my current career path it is not the most important.

As a result, I clicked on the four lines you see in the bottom right of the insert below. After clicking on it, I was able to move the school below the college where I got my B.A. and above my high school.

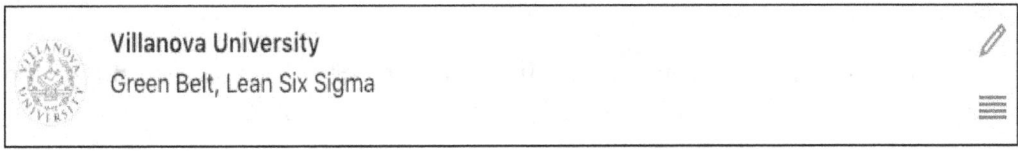

Use Your Educational Accomplishments to Boost Your Career

Another nice feature of the education section is how you can add additional information about your time in school.

As you can see below, I've added information about my speaking experience, since I would like to be called on for speaking engagements in the future.

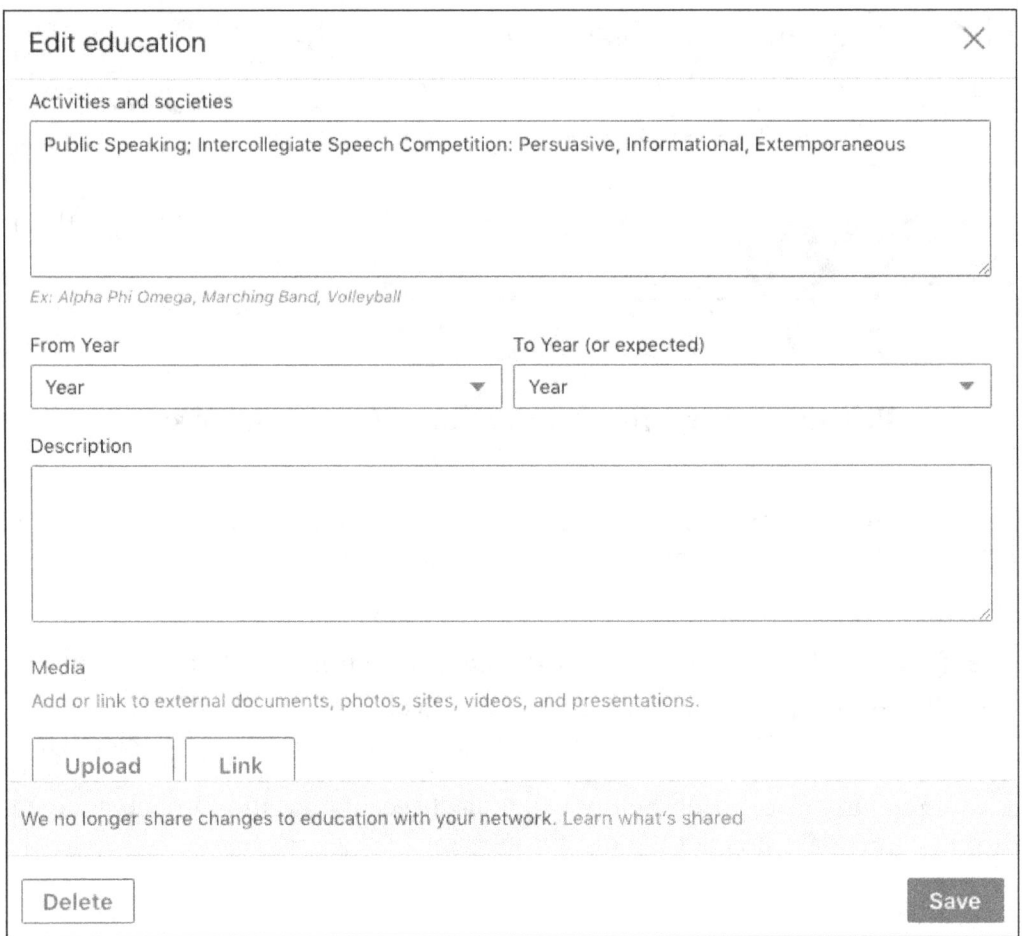

Depending on the type of education you've pursued, you may find it beneficial to enter a few words into the 'Description' field explaining your objective(s) in seeking this degree.

In addition, depending on your accomplishments in school, you may find your career will receive a boost if you upload or link to work that will be of interest to a potential employer.

Adding Years to Your Education

Unfortunately, with ageism an ongoing issue in candidate selection, consider this suggestion from The Muse regarding graduation dates:

"There's no rule that says you have to include the year you earned your degree at all, but the longest you'd want to keep that information is about 10 to 15 years, tops."

The Muse went onto share an interesting insight:

"There are always exceptions — particularly if you want to seem more experienced than your work history or appearance suggests...For example, if you've just finished school but have some decent work to speak of, removing your graduation date could help your chances of scoring an interview, as it'll help you to appear less green."[1]

Including Your High School

Most people will not expect you to list your high school. In fact, most people do not list their high school. The only exception may be if you haven't attained a higher level of education.

If you're pursuing a higher degree, be sure to add that school and your projected date of graduation. It means a great deal to any employer if they know you are working to improve yourself.

I've listed my high school because it was one of the happiest times in my life. In addition, I'm connected to a number of folks I went to school with, plus including the high school makes it easier for them to find me.

Because of the networking opportunity of potentially connecting with others you went to school with, adding your high school could prove to be a wise career move.

Additional Info in My Education Section

Because recruiters use complex searches known as 'Boolean' searches to find candidates, I've added 'Skills' and 'Technology' to my Education section.

Some might argue there's already a skills section. While this is true, there are limits to the number of skills that can be listed. LinkedIn informed me I can only list five more skills.

Adding 'Skills' and 'Technology' communicates my strengths while adding additional keywords. These additional keywords make my profile appear closer to the top of search results when Recruiters look for candidates with these strengths.

As mentioned above, it is wise to include common misspellings of your name because people will sometimes search for our names and misspell them. I placed mine at the end of my Education section.

Skills

- Budget development, tracking, outlooking
- Business Planning, revenue, market share, sales interlock
- Forecasting, revenue, expense, units
- IT Interface, business requirements creation, UAT, full implementation
- Knowledge Transfer, training, documentation, mentoring
- Presentation, creation, delivery to senior leadership, operations reviews
- Work analysis, auditing, improvement
- Project Management, cross-functional
- Results Reporting, dashboards, report development, analysis
- Special Bids
- Systems SME, mastering complexity
- Teaming
- Win/Loss analysis

Technology

- SAP Business Objects - Creating & Scheduling Queries in Webi
- Access: Creating Databases, Macros, Joins
- Excel: Macros, Pivot tables, Vlookups, Charts, Drop-downs, Conditional Formatting
- Word: Tables, Table of Contents, Training Documentation
- PowerPoint: I have received positive feedback for my crisp and clear presentations, particularly Operations Reviews
- Access: Intermediate

Common Misspellings

Fenical, Fenickle, Fenicle, Fenicol, Finical, Finickle, Finicle, Finicol, Finacal, Finackle, F Finacol, Financial

Are You Using Each LinkedIn Profile Section to Its Full Advantage?

Adding A Section to Your Profile

Because everyone has unique strengths and experiences, it is essential that you include all things that can help you achieve your career goals.

Sometimes that will mean adding a section that we haven't gone over yet. Here's how you can do this:

Below your headshot and headline, click on the white triangle next to 'Add profile section.'

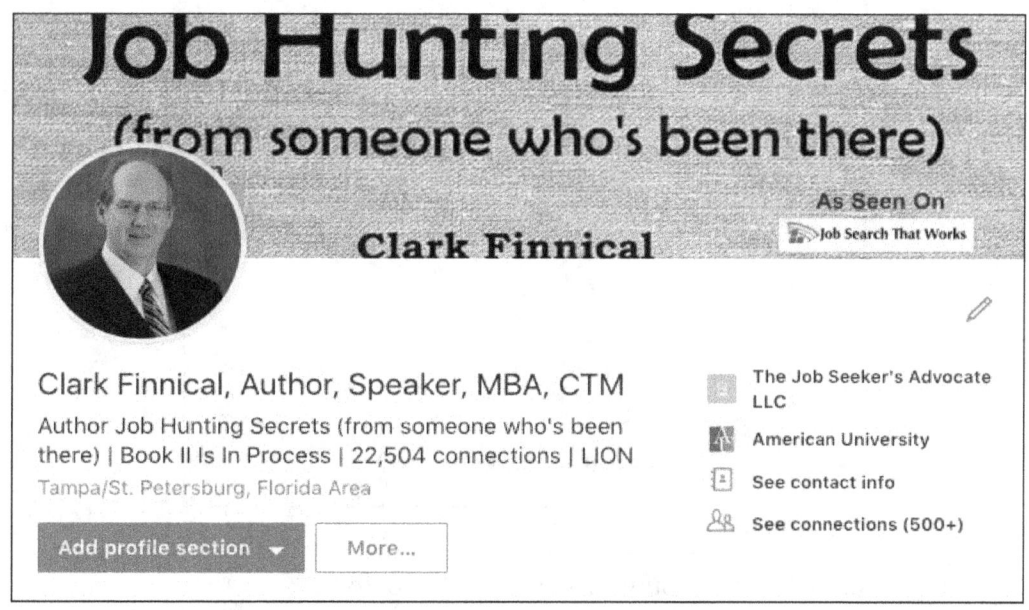

Directly underneath the 'Add profile section' tab you can choose between 'Background,' 'Skills,' 'Accomplishment's and, 'Additional Information' as you can see below. The options under 'Background' appear in the insert.

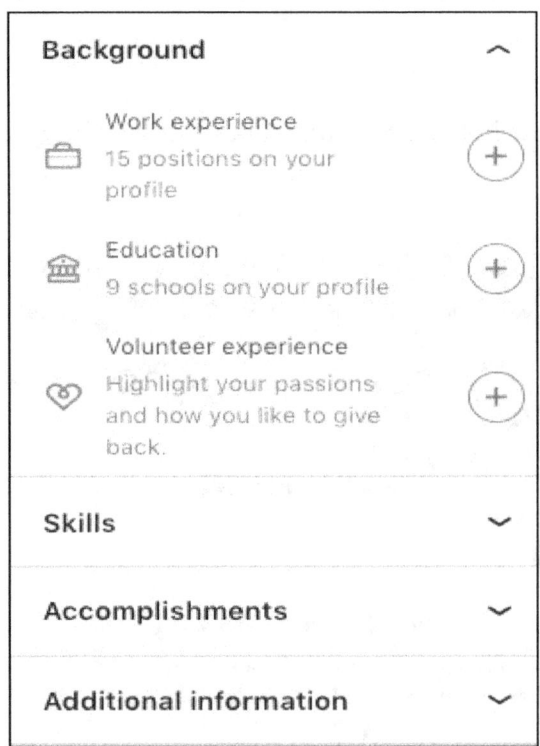

If you click 'Skills' you will see the insert below:

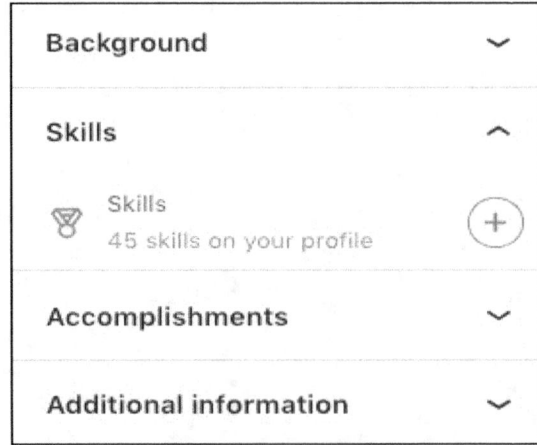

The third insert shows the sections under 'Accomplishments.'

Accomplishments ^

Publications
10 publications on your profile ⊕

Certifications
Members with a certification get 5x more profile views. ⊕

Patents
Showcase your innovation and expertise. ⊕

Courses
List coursework from your prior or continuing education. ⊕

Projects
Add compelling projects to demonstrate your experience. ⊕

Honors & Awards
2 honors & awards on your profile ⊕

Test Scores
4 test scores on your profile ⊕

Languages
Show how you can be a fit for a job or overseas opportunity. ⊕

Organizations
Show your involvement with communities that are important to you ⊕

If I click 'Additional Information,' I can request a recommendation from a connection.

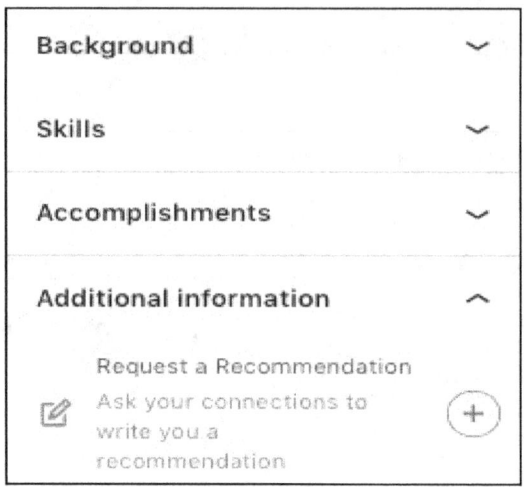

If, after reviewing all these options I decided I want to add a section under 'Language,' I would follow these steps:

Underneath my photo and headline, click 'Add profile section' > click 'Accomplishments' (I had to click 'Accomplishments' twice) > Scroll down to 'Languages' > click the circle with the
(+) plus symbol inside.

After clicking the circled plus symbol, the dialog box below opened. I entered 'English' and chose the correct proficiency. Then I clicked, 'Save.'

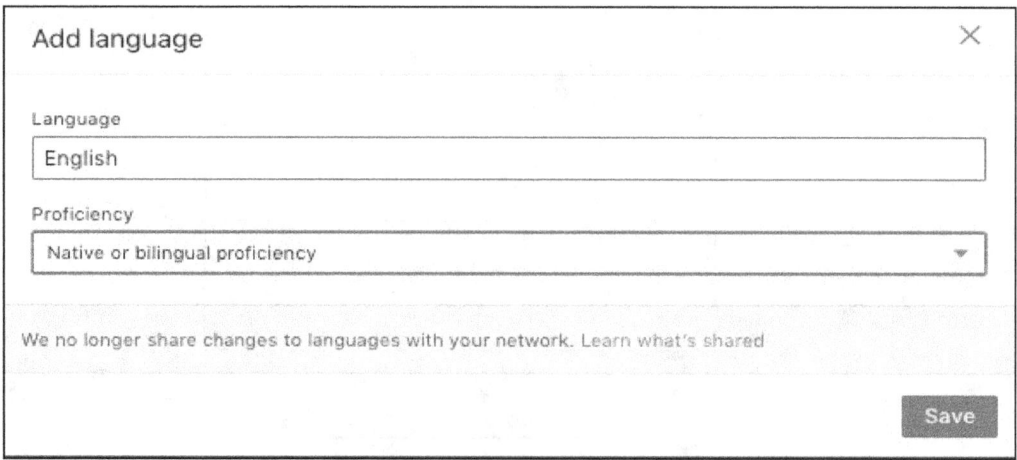

After clicking 'Save' the new information now appears in my Accomplishments section, as you can see here:

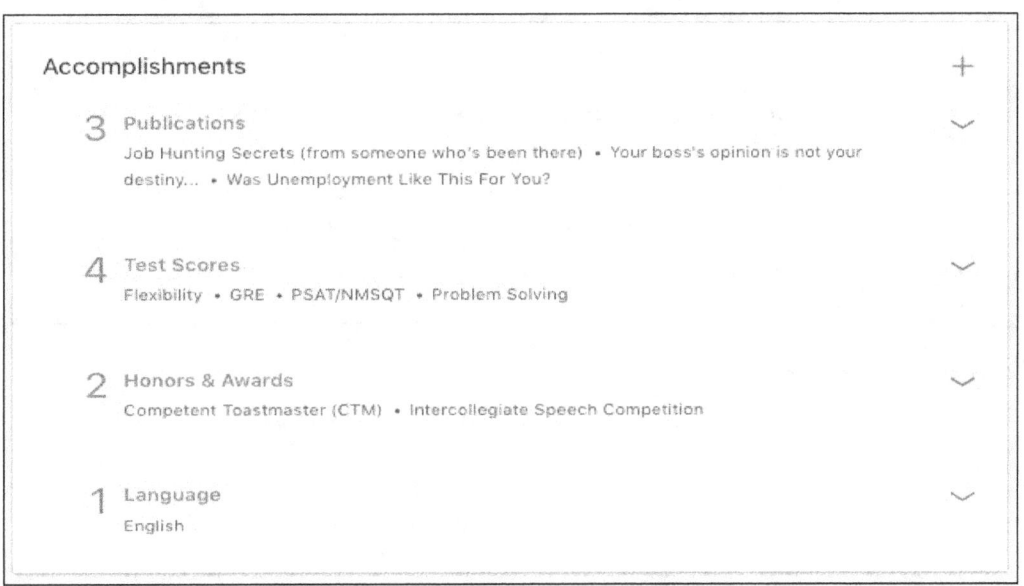

When you click on the drop-down arrow, you see additional detail. In the language section, clicking the drop down, reveals the language proficiency.

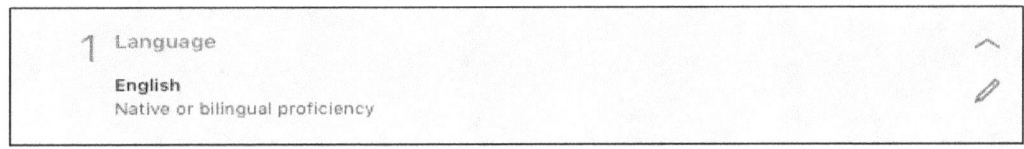

Follow the same process to add other sections to your profile.

Moving Information Within the Sections of Your LinkedIn Profile

While you can rearrange the order of entries for current positions, education and volunteer experience, you can't rearrange entire profile sections at least as of this printing.

For example, when I found my 'Author' experience wasn't at the top of my experience section, I selected the four lines below the 'pencil.' This enabled me to 'grab' that entry and take it to the top of my experience section.

It's a little tricky, by that I mean you may have to work with it because it tends to 'slide up and down' easily but it can be done.

Spicing Up Your LinkedIn Profile

How to Add Symbols to Your LinkedIn Profile

Many people add symbols to their profile to make it stand out.

I'm fond of using the large triangle bullet below to separate text in my profile.

▶

There are many different objects to choose from. Author and LinkedIn trainer Brynne Tillman wrote a 2014 post[1] entitled, "Symbols to Spice Up Your LinkedIn Profile."

In her post, Brynne shared how the value of symbols in a profile was debated, however she went on to say:

"I do believe if used well and sparingly, symbols have their place on the LinkedIn profile."[2]

Brynne's symbols can be accessed by clicking on this link:

https://www.linkedin.com/pulse/20140423001152-22901019-symbols-to-spice-up-your-linkedin-profile/

With LinkedIn You Can Search, Apply and Learn When Jobs Are Posted

To take advantage of these features click 'Jobs' at the top of the page.

Clicking 'Jobs' took me to the page below. Because I looked at a Senior Financial Analyst role at LinkedIn's CA HQ, LinkedIn's Jobs page is showing other CA-based FA roles.

Immediately below the CA-based roles, the Jobs page lists jobs local to the Tampa Bay area where I live. This information is provided automatically based on the information in my profile and my career interests. I have not updated my career interests.

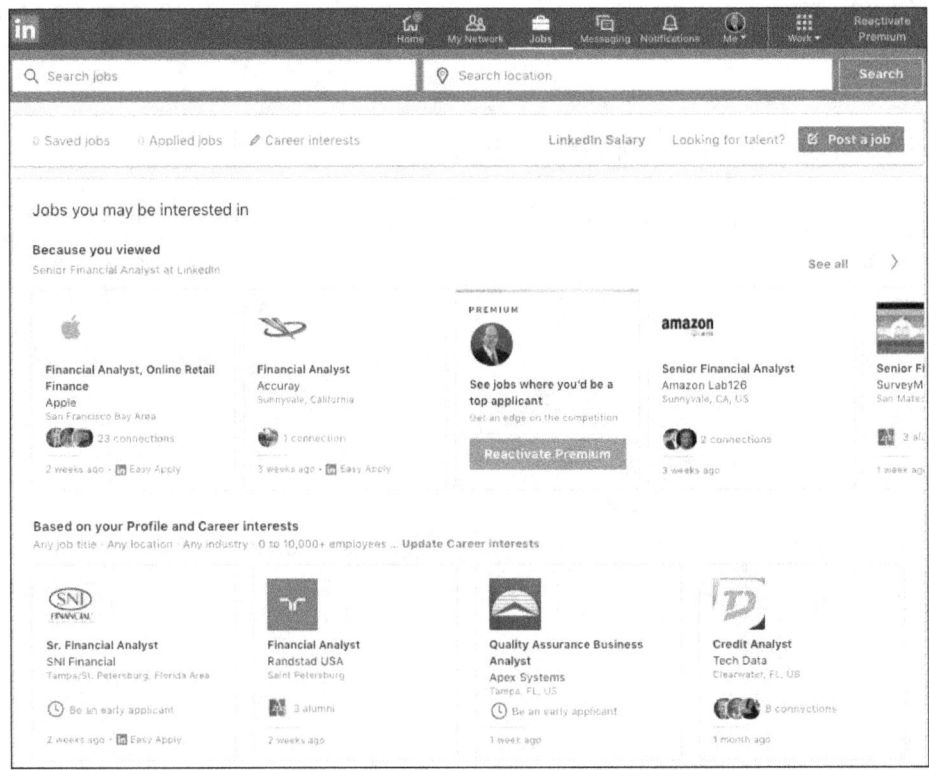

Career Interests

If you click on the 'Update Career Interests' link, you'll have the option to update your 'Privacy settings.'

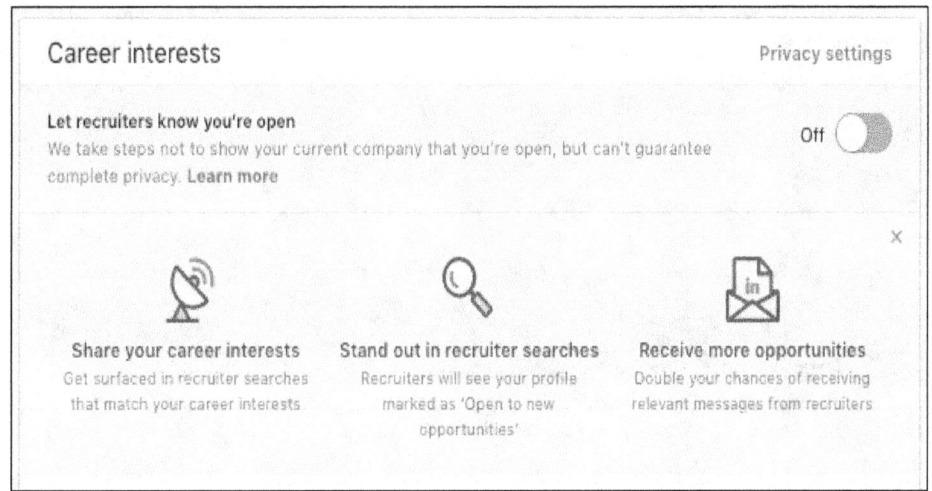

Before 'flicking' the toggle switch to 'On' to let recruiters know you're 'open' to other opportunities, it's important to understand the implications of making this choice.

When you click on the bolded 'Learn more' words above, LinkedIn takes you to a webpage with this verbiage:

> **Important:** In order to protect your privacy, we take steps to keep Recruiter users who work at your company, as well as related companies, from seeing the career interests that you share. Learn more about privacy for shared career interests and how to update your current company.

When you click on the bolded 'privacy for shared career interests,' LinkedIn provides a more detailed explanation.

Privacy for Shared Career Interests

Once you have **shared your career interests on LinkedIn**, users of LinkedIn's Recruiter product will be able to find you based on your shared career interests when they're searching for profiles.

Only recruiters who use LinkedIn's Recruiter product will have access to your preferences and career interest information. It won't be added to your LinkedIn.com profile.

In order to protect your privacy, we take steps to keep Recruiter users who work at your company, as well as related companies, from seeing the career interests that you share.

We do this by comparing a unique number (Company ID) assigned to the current employer listed on your profile with the Company ID for recruiters on our network. If a recruiter's Company ID is the same as the current employer listed on your profile, or the same as a company affiliated with that current employer based on our platform mapping, then we won't show your career interest preferences.

We cannot guarantee, however, that every company is accurately identified, or that affiliated companies are accurately mapped on our platform. We also cannot guarantee that every recruiter has an up-to-date and correct Company ID, so there's a small chance that your career interest preferences will be visible to a recruiter at your current employer or an affiliated company.

I've shared this information because I'd like you to understand the risks of using this LinkedIn feature.

Keep in mind, if someone at your current employer discovers that you are taking advantage of this LinkedIn feature, they could take actions which might not be good for your career!

Directly below the 'Career Interest Privacy' settings, you can answer a few questions which will help to determine the jobs that are recommended to you.

Your career interests help determine what jobs you're recommended.

Where are you in your search?

| Status | ▼ |

When would you like a new job?

| Start date | ▼ |

What job titles are you considering?

+ Add title

What locations would you work in?

+ Add location

What types of jobs are you open to?

☐ Full-time

☐ Contract

☐ Part-time

☐ Internship

☐ Remote

☐ Volunteer

☐ Temporary

Which industries do you prefer?

+ Add industry

What size company would you like to work for? (Number of employees)

| 1 ▼ | to | 10,000+ ▼ |

In order to illustrate what the Jobs section can do, I've made the selections you can see in the insert below.

Where are you in your search?
Actively applying ▼

When would you like a new job?
As soon as possible ▼

What job titles are you considering?
+ Financial|

Financial Analyst

Financial Advisor

Chief **Financial** Officer

Financial Assistant

Financial Controller

Senior **Financial** Analyst

As soon as I finished typing 'Financial,' it began to populate the titles you see above.

As you can see in the insert below, I made these selections.

Job Titles: 'Financial Analyst,' 'Senior Financial Analyst' and 'Financial Analysis Manager.'

Work Location: 'Tampa/St. Petersburg,' 'Florida area.'

Job Type: 'Full-time.'

Industry: 'Hospital & Health Care.'

Company size: '1 to 10,000+.'

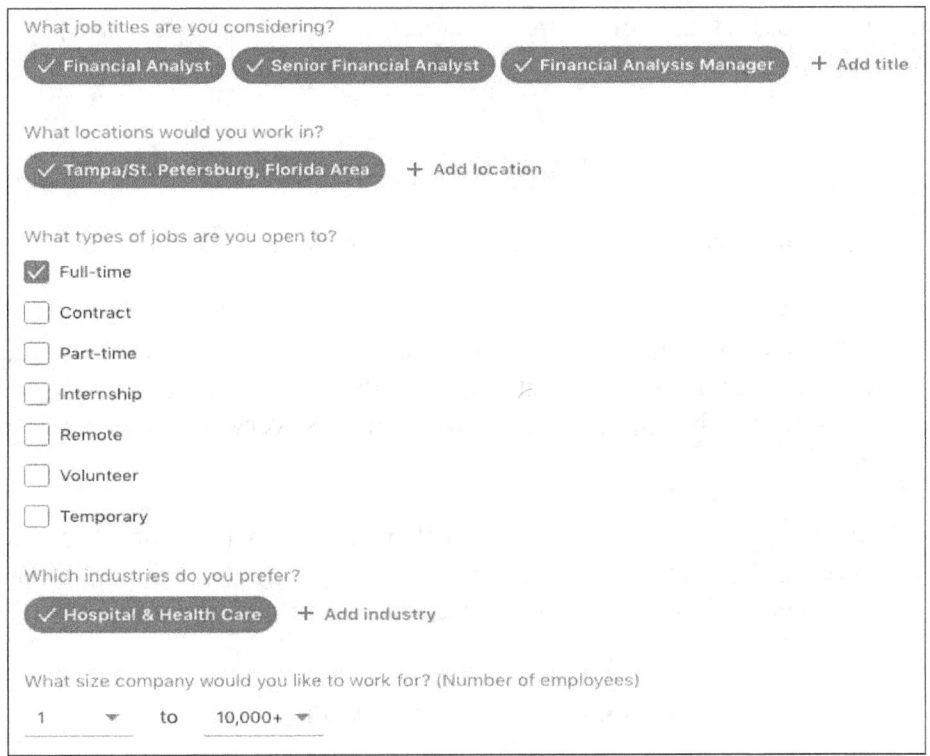

After making the selections, I clicked the 'Go to Jobs' link directly below the 'Career Interests.'

Here are the jobs LinkedIn identified:

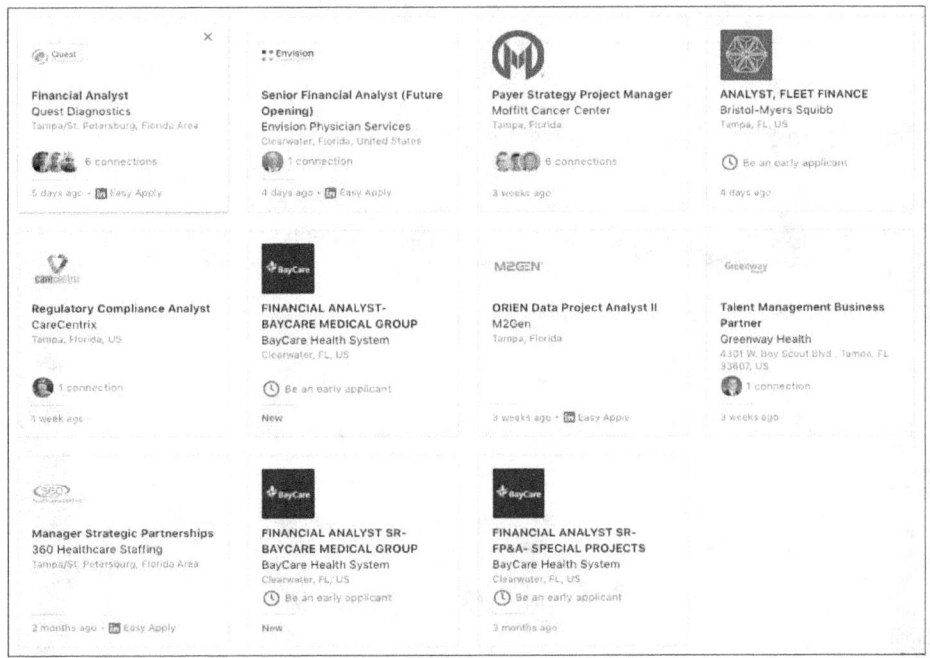

LinkedIn provides the following valuable information that will help you in your job search.

Age of Job Posting

The wisest thing you can do is apply to the newest roles. Why?

- Being first or among the first to apply for a position can make a big difference. It makes you stand out. It also communicates you are very interested in this specific position. That is very important to any hiring manager.

- Even though the other jobs are still posted, you have no idea where those companies are in their hiring process. It could be they've already found someone and they just haven't gotten around to taking the job down.

Connections Who Work There

According to Jobvite, 39.9% of all new hires are referrals. If you're connected to employees at companies where you are applying, one or more of these people could be a referral.

After I reviewed the 11 jobs above, I scrolled down the page and found this link:

Search for more jobs

After clicking that link, the message below appears.

I clicked 'Try it now' and the webpage below appeared. As you can see, it provided information in a different format. In addition, it returned 227 results.

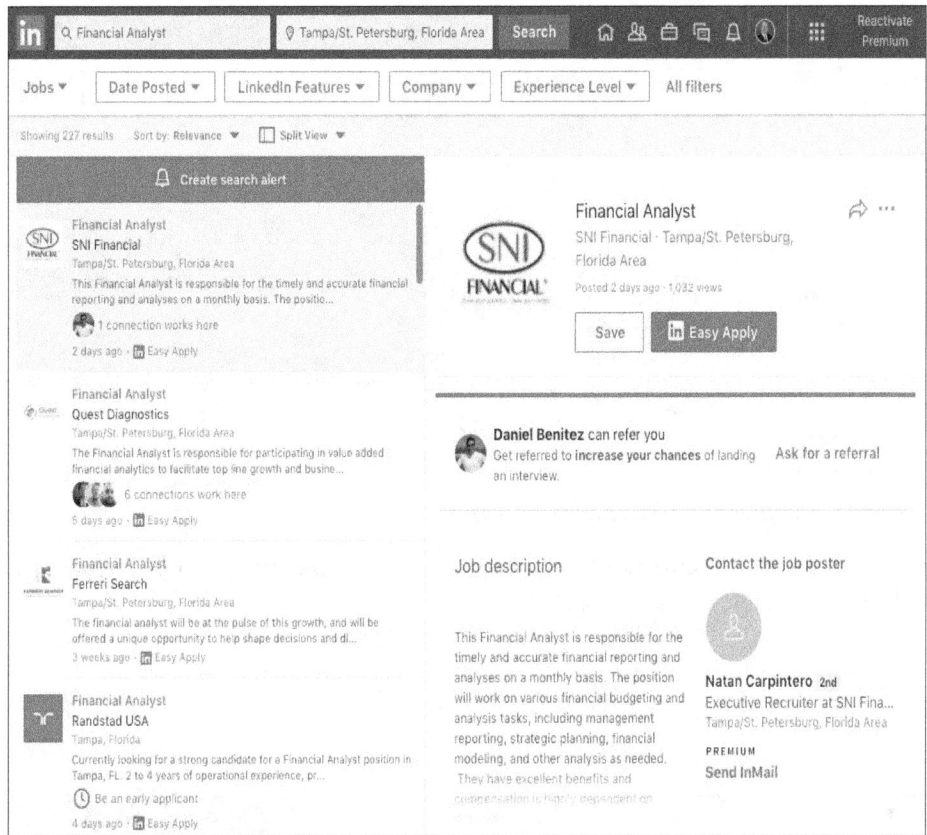

You can click the drop down next to the 'Split view' option (near the top of the screen) to see the 'Classic view,' which is basically the same information but in a different layout, if that is your preference.

I recommend clicking the 'All jobs filters' link so you can easily filter out those jobs that are not a good match.

After clicking that link, I made the choices below and clicked the 'Apply' tab.

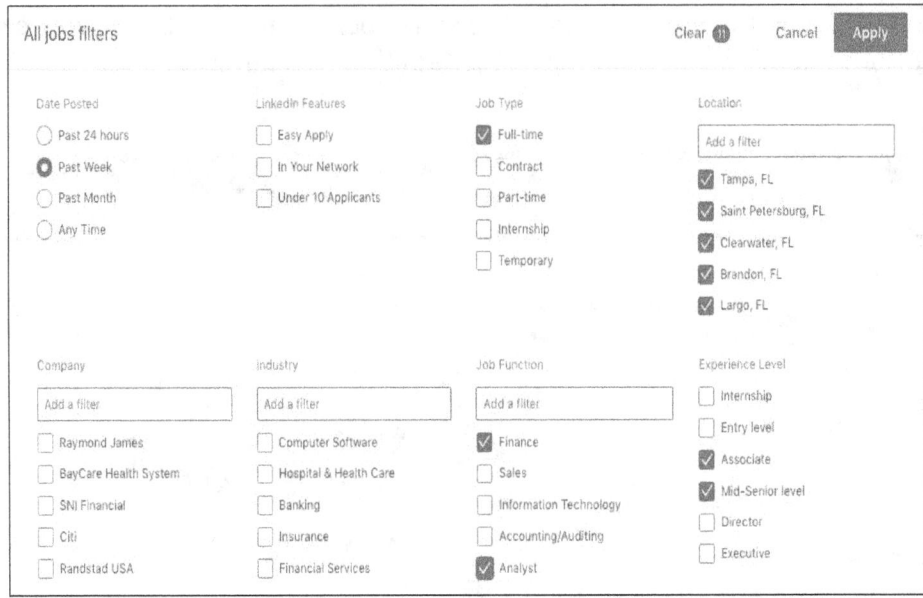

I appreciated the 'Date posted' filter the most, as my greatest chances are with those roles that are newest.

See the insert below.

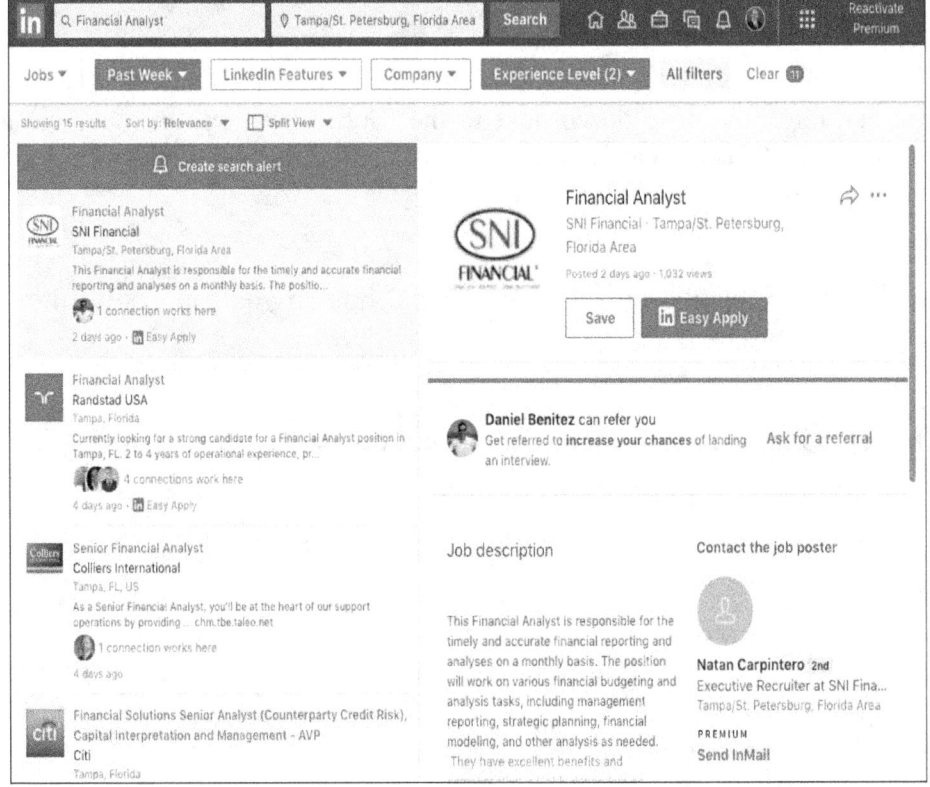

Talentworks analyzed 1,600 job applications to determine the chance of getting an interview based on the number of days between application submittal and job posting.

Applications submitted between 2-4 days after a job is posted, have up to an 8x higher chance of getting an interview, even if the same application is being submitted.[1]

LinkedIn Features

The LinkedIn Features option may prove very helpful in your job search.

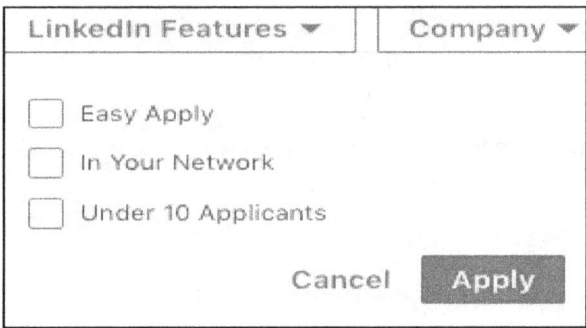

Easy Apply

When I selected the 'Easy apply' option and clicked the 'Easy apply' button on one of the jobs that was returned, the dialog box below appeared.

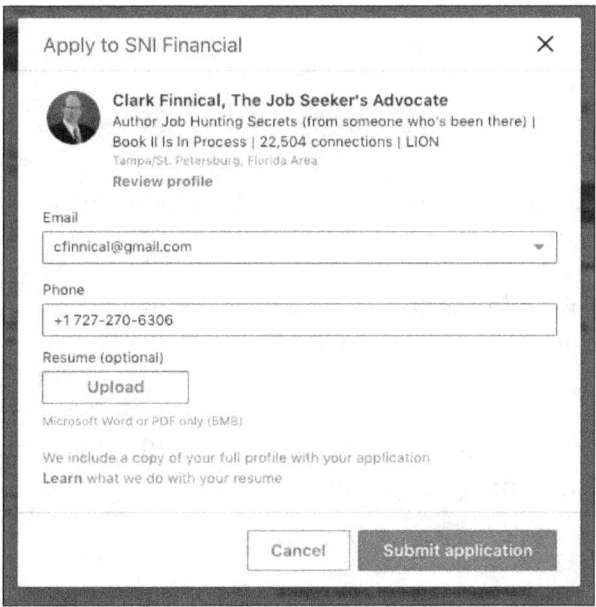

After you click 'Submit application,' LinkedIn sends a copy of your full profile along with your contact information to the employer. So, you'd want to ensure your profile is ready to be sent before you do this and a good email is loaded in your contacts.

You also have the option of uploading a copy of your resume which I strongly recommend. Practically everyone ever involved in the candidate selection process is accustomed to having an applicant's resume, so ignoring this step could sink your chances no matter how good your profile is.

For more information on creating a winning resume, see my first book, Job Hunting Secrets (from someone who's been there.)

In Your Network

Narrowing your job search to companies where your LinkedIn connections work makes it much easier for anyone searching for a referral.

Under 10 Applicants

I'm not certain the 'Under 10 applicants' option is exactly what it says it is. I say that because the same role will be posted on the company's career site and most likely on Indeed as well.

The best way to identify roles with few applicants is to set up a job alert in LinkedIn, or on the employer's web site so that you're are notified as soon as the role is posted.

Creating Job Alerts

I strongly recommend creating a 'Job alert' in LinkedIn.

If you're thinking why bother, I already have an Indeed job alert as well as job alerts with multiple companies, consider the following.

Companies pay to post their positions on LinkedIn, therefore these companies are eager to fill these roles as quickly as possible.

I am not saying you shouldn't create job alerts at Indeed or with the companies you are interested in. You should do that because not every company will post its jobs on LinkedIn.

To create a 'Job alert.'

1. Click on the brief case symbol at the top of the screen;

2. Enter as many filters as you'd like. In the insert below, I added 'Financial Analyst' and 'Tampa/St. Petersburg, Florida Area;'

3. Click on 'Create search alert;'

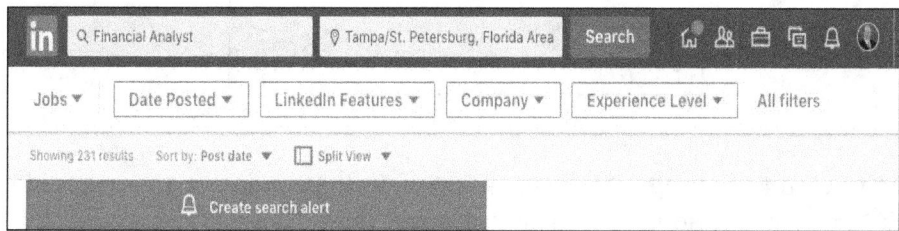

4. Choose how often you'd like to receive alerts, as well as how you'd like to be notified.

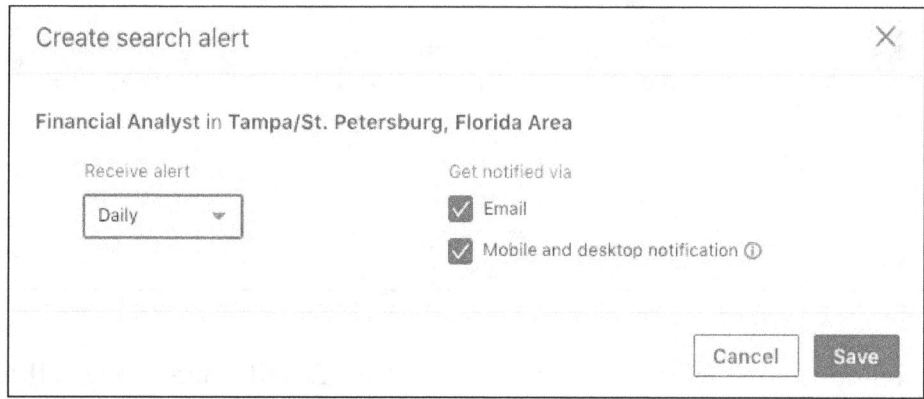

After creating your job alert, it's always a good idea to review your communication settings to make sure you'll receive your job alerts.

Do this by going to the LinkedIn home page > clicking your picture at the top of the screen then 'Settings & Privacy.'

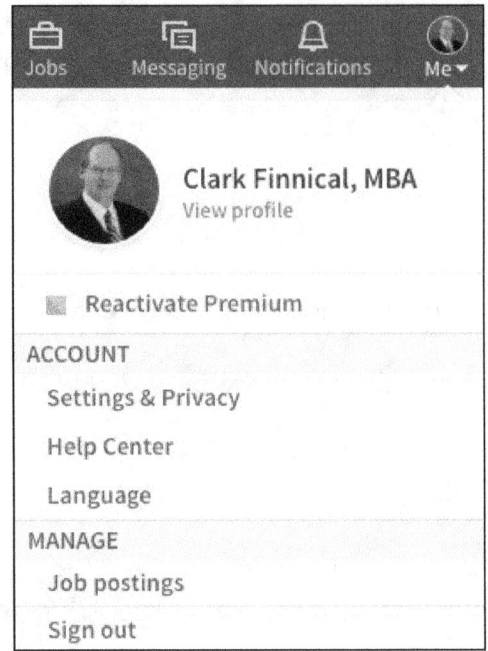

After clicking 'Settings & Privacy,' you will be taken to a page like you see below. Click 'Communications' and 'Email frequency.'

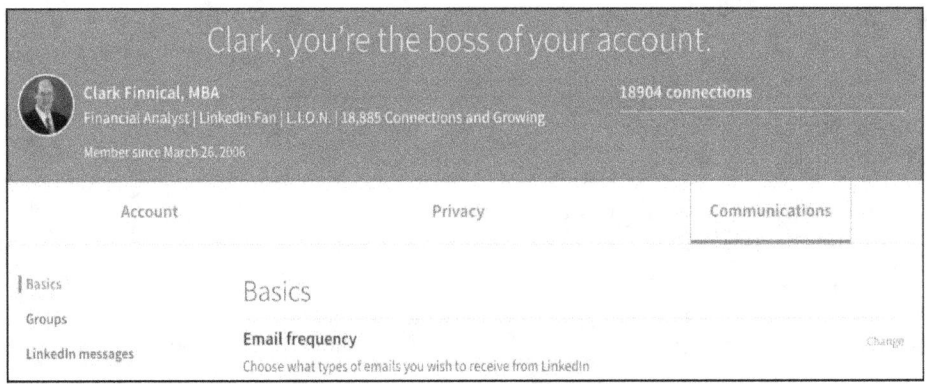

Scroll down to 'Jobs and opportunities' Select 'Details' and change all 'Off - On' selections to the 'On' position. LinkedIn then saves your choices.

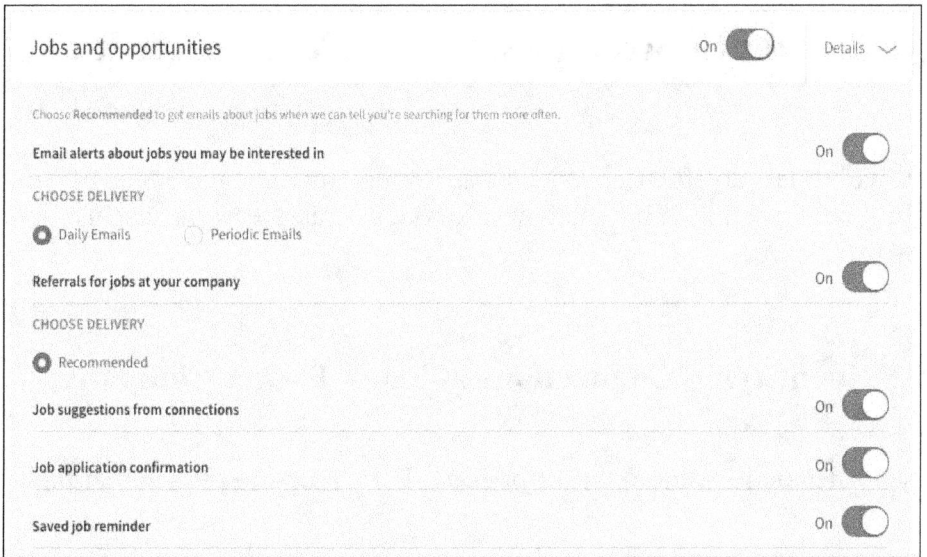

Jobs and opportunities   On ⬤ Details ⌄

Choose **Recommended** to get emails about jobs when we can tell you're searching for them more often.

Email alerts about jobs you may be interested in   On ⬤

CHOOSE DELIVERY

⬤ Daily Emails   ○ Periodic Emails

Referrals for jobs at your company   On ⬤

CHOOSE DELIVERY

⬤ Recommended

Job suggestions from connections   On ⬤

Job application confirmation   On ⬤

Saved job reminder   On ⬤

LinkedIn Strategies to Land Your Next Job

So far, we've largely focused on getting found, making the most of your profile, and using LinkedIn's Jobs section. This chapter addresses strategies you can use to network your way into a new role.

Identifying Connections at Your Target Company

Let's say I decided I want to work for IBM. If I wanted to pursue that path, here's what I would do.

I'd go to the top of the LinkedIn page, place the cursor in the search bar and click 'People.'

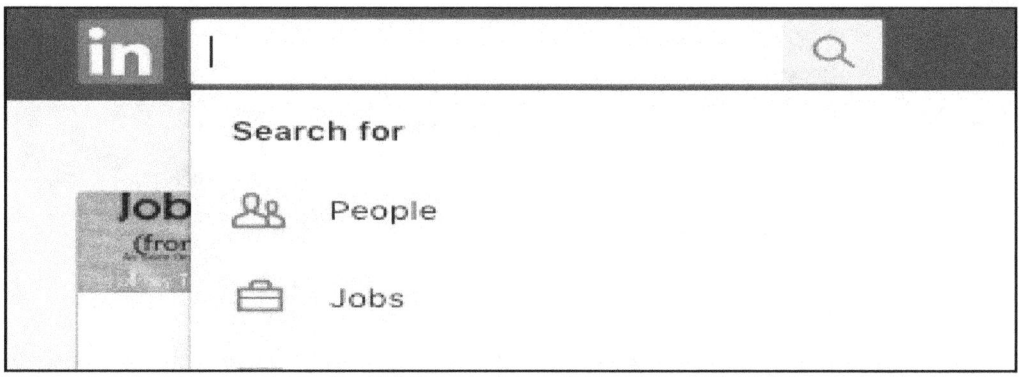

Next, I'd click 'All Filters.'

After clicking 'All Filters,' under 'Connections' I'd select '1st' because those are the people I'm directly connected with.

Next, because I am interested in IBM, I'd select 'IBM' under 'Current companies' and 'IBM' under 'Past companies.'

I'd then click the blue 'Apply' button.

Connections of	Locations	Current companies
Add connection of	Add a location	Add a company
	☐ United States	☐ Amazon
	☐ India	☐ Google
	☐ Tampa/St. Petersburg, Florida Area	☑ IBM
	☐ United Arab Emirates	☐ Microsoft
	☐ Greater New York City Area	☐ University of South Florida

Past companies	Industries	Profile language
Add a company	Add an industry	☐ English
☑ IBM	☐ Think Tanks	☐ Spanish
☐ US Army	☐ Human Resources	☐ French
☐ Microsoft	☐ Information Technology and Services	☐ Portuguese
☐ Citi		☐ German
☐ Accenture	☐ Staffing and Recruiting	
	☐ Marketing and Advertising	

After clicking the blue 'Apply' button, 20 connections were returned who currently work for IBM, or had worked for IBM in the past.

People ▼   Locations ▼   1st ▼   IBM ▼   All Filters   Clear ③

Think in Systems? - Earn a Systems Design Certificate from Cornell. All Online. Ap|

Showing 20 results

1st
Cloud Managed Application Services Market Leader - North America Sales- Com...   Message
Tampa/St. Petersburg, Florida Area
Current: Cloud Managed Application Services Market Leader - North America Sales-
Communications /CSI at IBM
81 shared connections

• 1st
Design Principal for Discovery Strategy: IA, Content & Data Visualization   Message
Greater Denver Area
Current: Design Principal for Discovery Strategy: IA, Content & Data Visualization at IBM
14 shared connections

• 1st in
Distinguished Engineer, Director, Chief Architect- Analytics, Data Governance & I...   Message
Dallas/Fort Worth Area
Current: Director & Distinguished Engineer - Information Integration and Governance at IBM
34 shared connections

Armed with this information, I can now reach out to these folks and, see if we can help each other. Don't look for the other person to think of how you can help him. Read their profile and google their name to see if there isn't something you could help them with.

Since 39.9% of all new hires are referrals, this is well worth your effort.

Do Your Close Contacts Have Connections at Your Target Company?

Since, we are not equally close to all our connections, it can be valuable to examine the connections of those we are closest to. Here's how you can do that:

As we did before, go to the top of the LinkedIn page, place the cursor in the search bar and click 'People.'

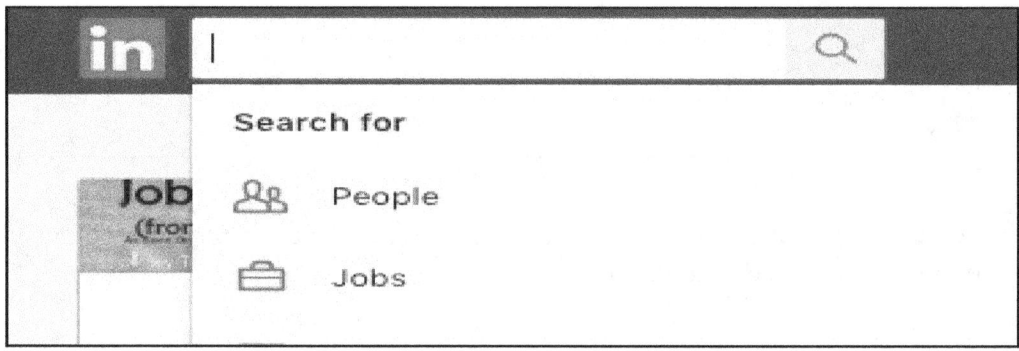

Next, click 'All Filters.'

Next, enter a connection's name in the 'Connections of' field. As you can see below, once you start typing the first name of your 1st level connection, LinkedIn displays all of your 1st level connections with that first name.

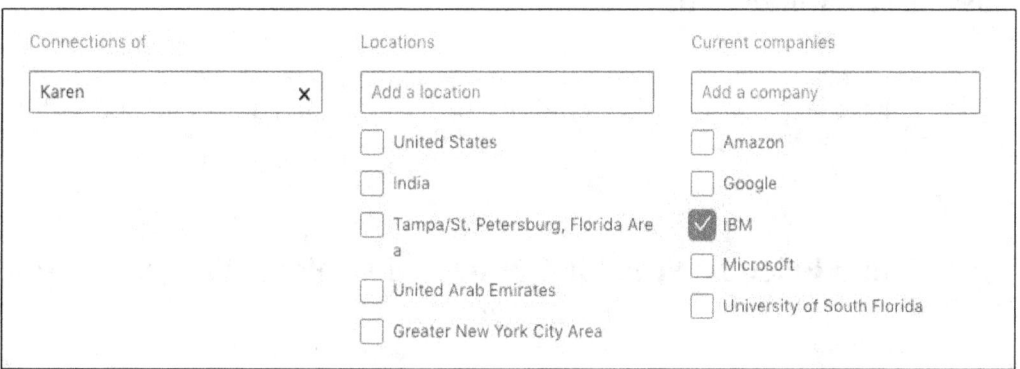

All people filters

First name | Company | Connections
[   ] | [   ] | ☐ 1st

Last name | School | ☐ 2nd
[   ] | [   ] | ☐ 3rd+

Title
[   ]

Connections of | Locations | Current companies
[Karen   ×] | [Add a location   ] | [Add a company   ]

Karen ▓▓▓ 1st | ☐ United States | ☐ Amazon
Manager - Network of Profession... | ☐ India | ☐ Google

Karen • 1st | ☐ Tampa/St. Petersburg, Florida Area | ☐ IBM
Recruiting Professional 12,000+ d... | | ☐ Microsoft

Karen • 1st | ☐ United Arab Emirates | ☐ University of South Florida
Health / Life / Medicare... |

Karen • 1st | ☐ Greater New York City Area
Account Manager at |

Industries | Profile language

After entering my connection's name, I go to 'Current companies' and check 'IBM' because I'd like to see if she has any connections who currently work there.

Connections of | Locations | Current companies
[Karen   ×] | [Add a location   ] | [Add a company   ]

| ☐ United States | ☐ Amazon
| ☐ India | ☐ Google
| ☐ Tampa/St. Petersburg, Florida Area | ☑ IBM
| | ☐ Microsoft
| ☐ United Arab Emirates | ☐ University of South Florida
| ☐ Greater New York City Area |

After I click 'Apply,' I found my friend has 232 connections that currently work at IBM.

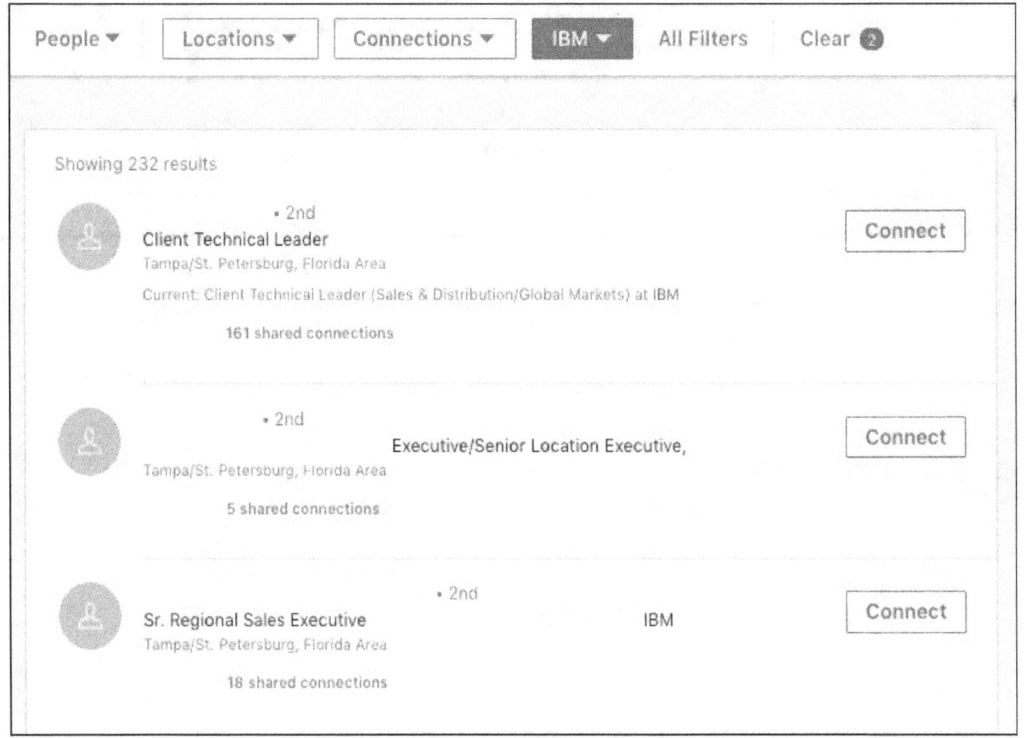

At this point, if I was actively searching for a new role, I would contact my friend to discuss where I'd like to work at IBM. I would also see which friend is best suited to connect me with the right person.

This is a tremendous strategy because the average person does not remember everyone they've ever worked with.

By taking these steps, you will remind her of these connections and she in turn can then help you.

If You or Your Friends Are Not Connected to Your Target Company's Employees...

Let's say, I'm interested in working for SAS, a leader in Analytics Software, headquartered in Cary, NC.

As I did before, I went to the top of the LinkedIn page, placed the cursor in the search bar and clicked 'People.'

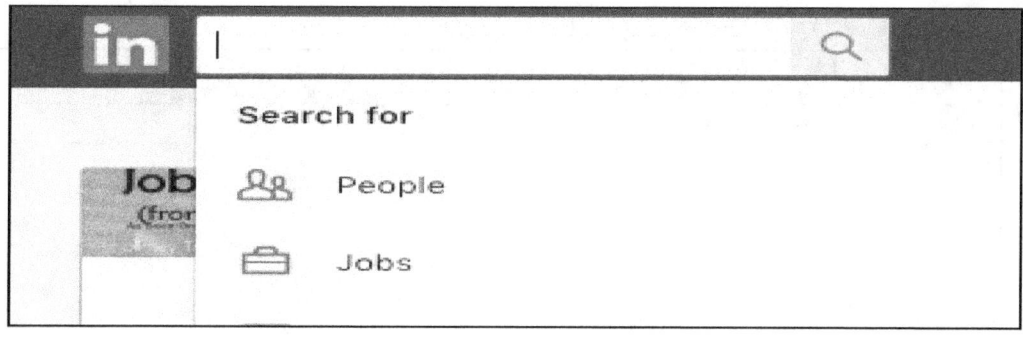

Next, I clicked 'All Filters.'

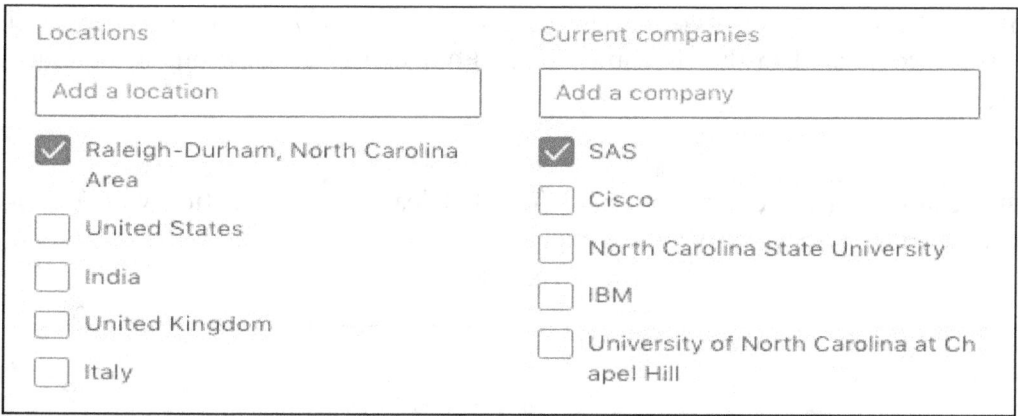

I entered 'SAS' into the 'Current companies' field. Because I am interested in working at their headquarters, I entered 'Raleigh-Durham' into the 'Locations' field.

Locations	Current companies
Add a location	Add a company
☑ Raleigh-Durham, North Carolina Area	☑ SAS
☐ United States	☐ Cisco
☐ India	☐ North Carolina State University
☐ United Kingdom	☐ IBM
☐ Italy	☐ University of North Carolina at Chapel Hill

After clicking 'Apply,' 5,000+ names were returned. While I could contact some of these folks, I knew my odds of networking myself into a job would increase if I was able to leverage some common bonds.

Using Connections from Your Former Employer

I, then instructed LinkedIn, to show me of those 5000+ names how many of them previously worked for my former employer. I did that by entering 'Avaya' into the 'Past companies' field.

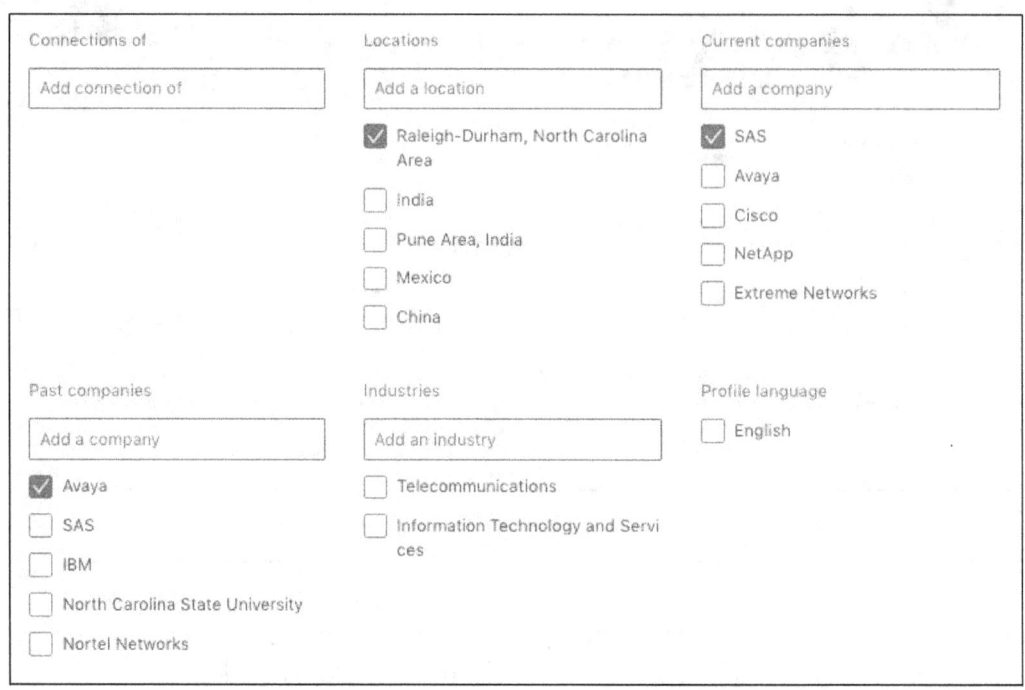

After clicking 'Apply,' two names were returned. As you can see below, nine of my connections are connected to the first individual. Four of my connections are connected to the second individual.

After examining these connections, I found at least one connection who I believe would introduce me to these SAS employees if I wanted to pursue this career.

Using Connections from College

If I wasn't able to leverage connections from my former employer, I'd see if I could leverage connections from college.

I would do this by unchecking 'Avaya' from 'Past companies.' I would then enter 'Wake Forest University' in the 'Schools' section as I attended Wake during my freshman and sophomore years.

32 members were returned. After reviewing the shared connections, I found one connection who could introduce me to an SAS employee, if I was truly interested.

Uncover the Value of Your Existing Connections

How to Export Your Connections' Contact Info

Your first question might be, "Why would I do that?"

There's a lot of value in your connections that you probably don't even realize.

This exercise will illustrate my point.

Click the 'My Network' icon at the top of the LinkedIn page.

Click 'See all.'

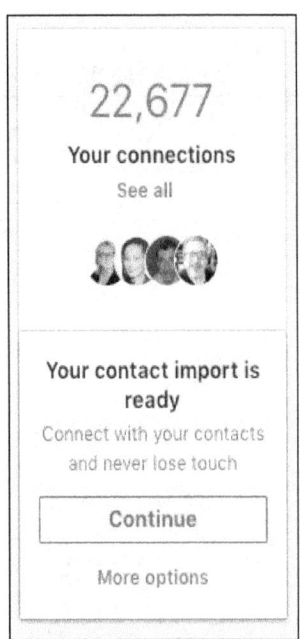

Click 'Manage synced and imported contacts.'

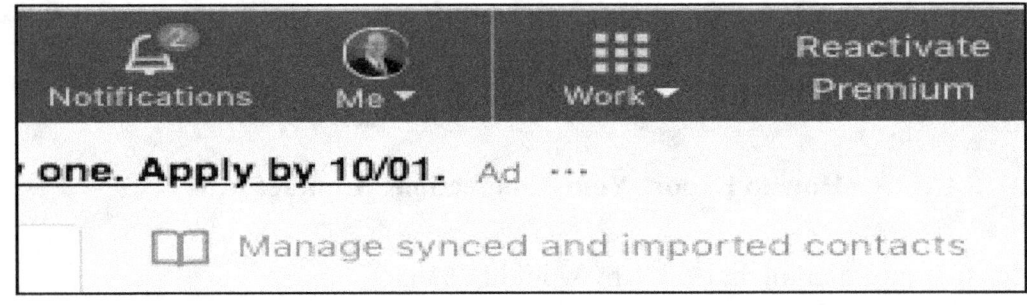

Under Advanced Actions > Click 'Export contacts.'

Under 'Download your data' > Click 'Pick and choose' > 'Connections' > 'Request archive.'

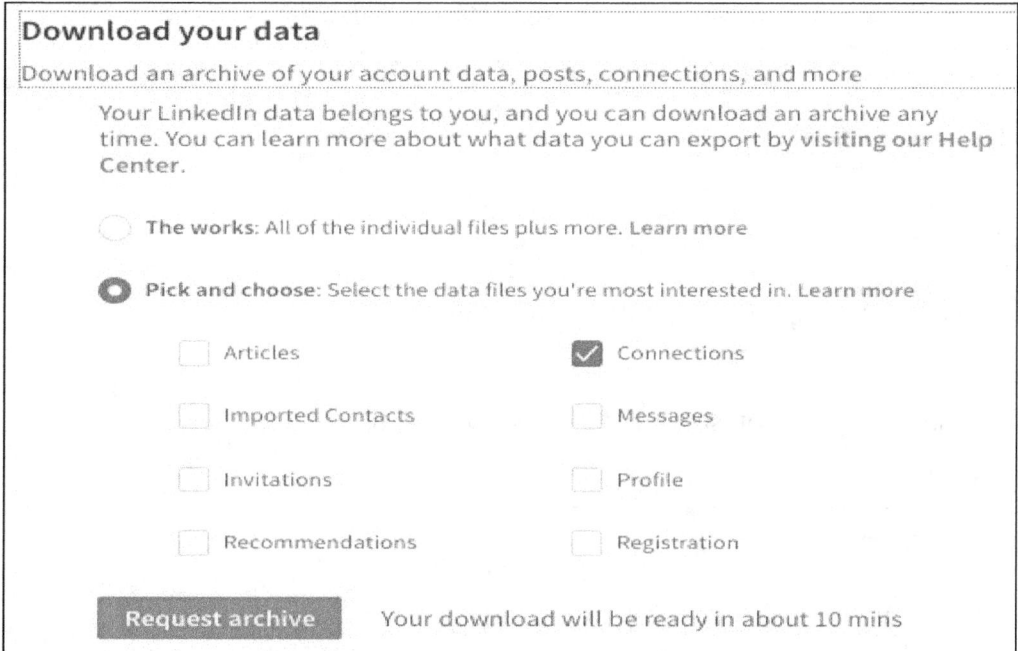

In about 10 minutes, you will receive an email that looks like this:

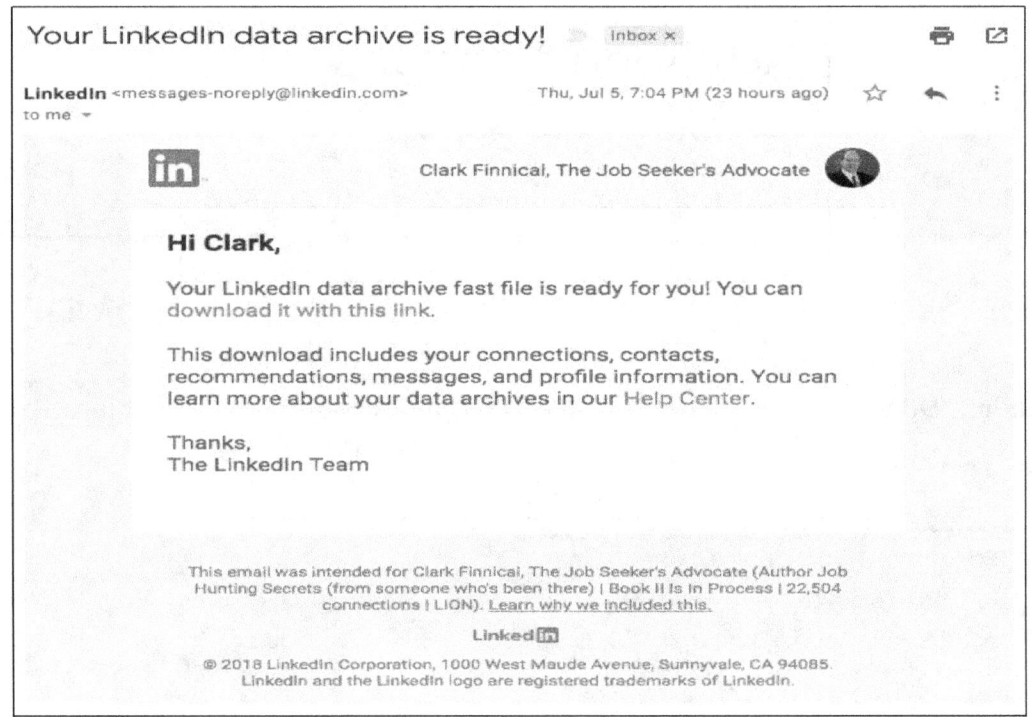

Click where it says, 'download it with this link.'

This opens the page you see below. Click 'Download archive.'

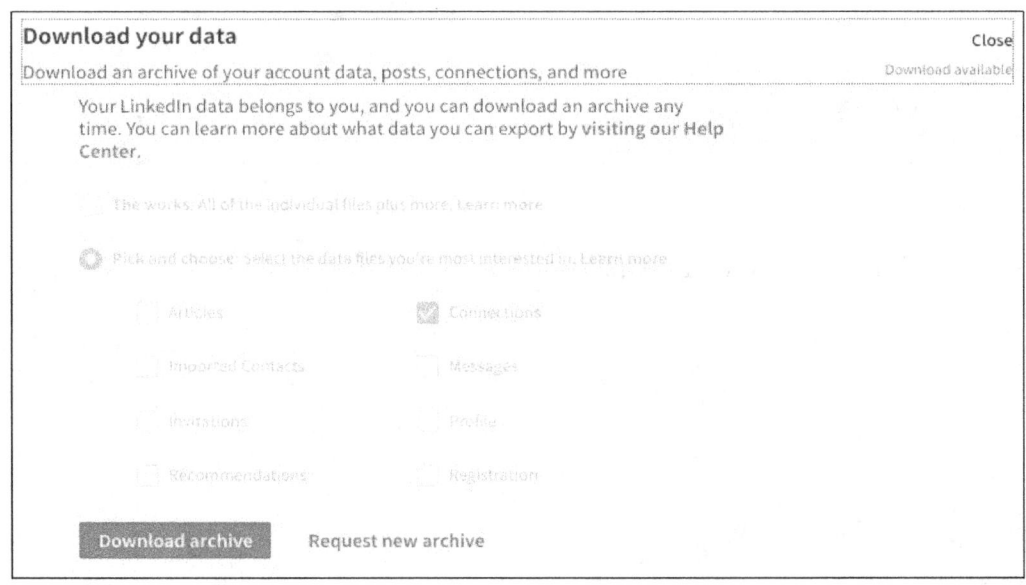

After clicking 'Download archive,' you'll be prompted to save the zipped file as you see here.

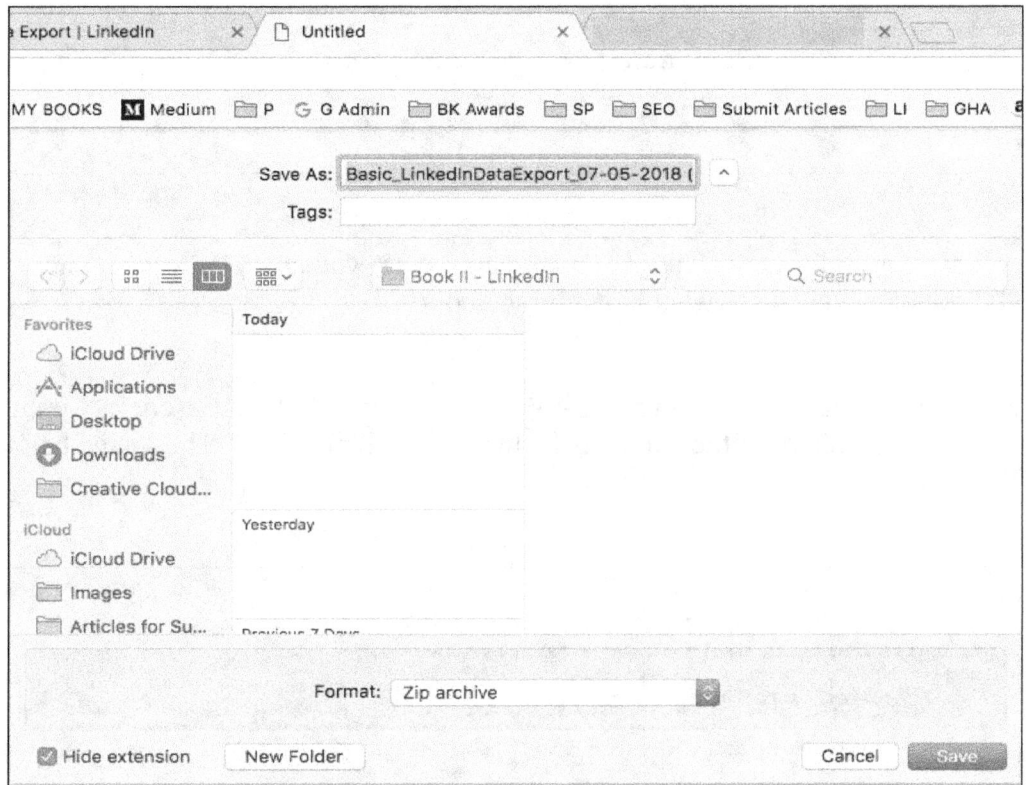

Open the file to access the CSV file. Save it to your Mac or PC.

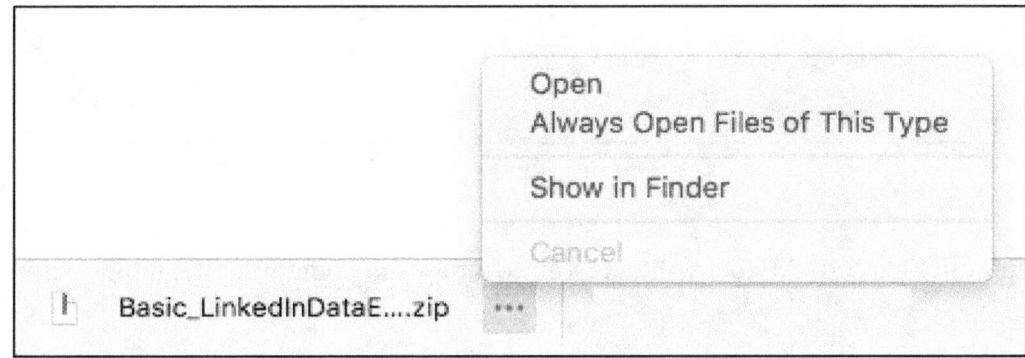

Within Excel go to the folder with the CSV file and open it.

When you look at the file and expand the columns it will look like the insert below:

	A	B	C	D	E	F
1	First Name	Last Name	Email Address	Company	Position	Connected On
2	Brent		@yahoo.com	De La Pena & Holiday	Managing Partner (Tampa)	3/16/13, 4:05 PM
3	Michael		@changetheworld.com	SocialMediopolis.com	Entrepreneur | Social Entrepreneur | Publisher | Advertising and Marketing Exec	3/14/13, 11:33 AM
4	Craig		@SHiFTSelling.com	SHiFT Selling, Inc.	Speaker, Advisor, Trainer, & Mentor	4/15/13, 6:37 AM
5	Arvell		@yahoo.com	Encode Entertainment LLC	Executive Producer / Director	7/14/13, 8:35 PM

At first this information might not seem very valuable, however once you start manipulating the data, you'll see what I'm talking about.

Here's what I did in a few minutes – With the Excel file Open > click 'Command' – A (ctrl-A for PC's) to select all of the data. Click 'Insert' > 'Pivot Table.' The image below appears > click 'OK'

Create PivotTable

Choose the data that you want to analyze.

○ Select a table or range

Table/Range: 'Connections 2'!$A$1:$F$21538

○ Use an external data source

Choose Connection... No data fields have been retrieved.

Choose where to place the PivotTable.

● New worksheet
○ Existing worksheet

Table/Range:

Cancel | OK

After clicking 'OK,' Excel will take you to a new tab containing the tables below.

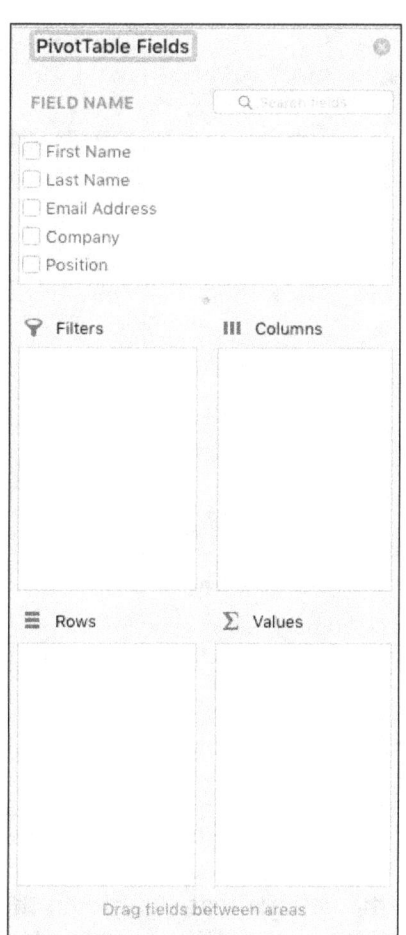

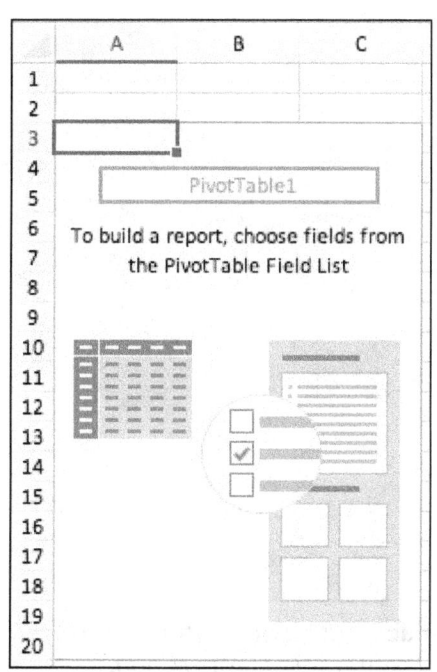

	A	B	C
1			
2			
3			
4			
5	PivotTable1		
6	To build a report, choose fields from		
7	the PivotTable Field List		
8			
9			
10			
11			
12			
13			
14			
15			
16			
17			
18			
19			
20			

When you follow the steps below, you'll begin to see the value of the data. Move the 'Company field' to the 'Rows' section > Move 'Last Name' to the 'Values' section. (If it says 'Sum,' right click on it > click 'Field settings' and choose 'Summarize by Count' as you see here.

Next, go to the newly created table on the left > place your cursor in column B under the 'Count' column > Right click > 'Sort' > 'Sort Largest to Smallest,' as you see below.

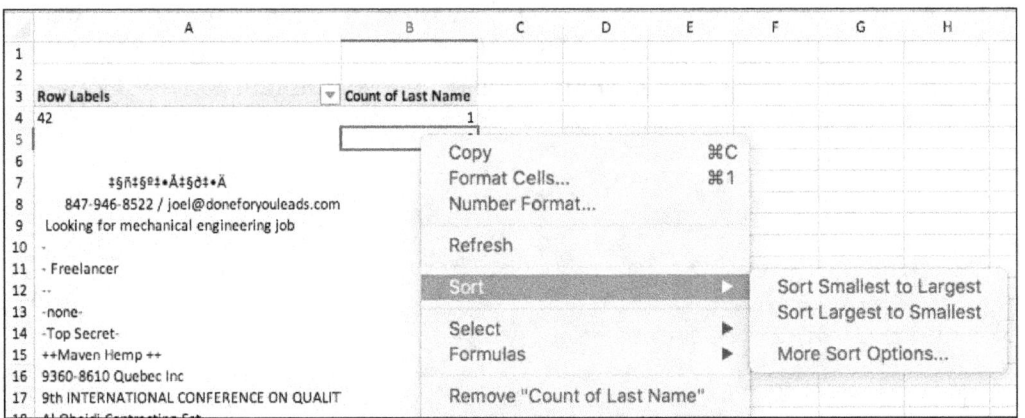

After you follow the steps above, your pivot table will look something like the one below. I've intentionally included a large portion of my pivot table so you can start to see the value.

3	Row Labels	▾↓	Count of Last Name
4	(blank)		331
5	Avaya		162
6	Self-employed		160
7	Self Employed		80
8	Confidential		58
9			47
10	IBM		42
11	LeadGenius		38
12	Freelance		35
13	Oracle		33
14	Cisco		28
15	Accenture		28
16	Kforce Inc		26
17	Citi		26
18	Amazon		23
19	Microsoft		22
20	Retired		21
21	Freelancer		21
22	PwC		20
23	Bank of America		20
24	Apple		19
25	Capgemini		18
26	Wells Fargo		17
27	Self		17
28	Upwork		17
29	Robert Half		17
30	Facebook		17
31	Cognizant		17
32	ADP		17
33	EY		16
34	Google		15
35	Salesforce		14
36	Deloitte		14
37	Verizon		13

Let's say, I'm interested in working for Ernst and Young (EY). The beauty of pivot tables is I can double click on the '16' next to EY and get the names, titles, dates connected and emails for all of the connections I have that work for EY.

	A	B	C	D	E	F
1	First Name	Last Name	Email Address	Company	Position	Connected On
2	Mert		?gmail.com	EY	Audit Intern	11/4/17, 2:37 PM
3	Robert		.edu	EY	Senior Associate - Transaction Real Estate	11/24/16, 5:32 PM
4	Rohan			EY	Assurance Services	3/1/17, 6:48 PM
5	Giri Neekish		il.com	EY	Senior Consultant	3/15/15, 4:38 AM
6	Priyam		27@gmail.com	EY	Associate Consultant	3/3/17, 3:54 AM
7	Sierra		nail.com	EY	Senior Consultant	2/4/14, 7:07 PM
8	David		du	EY	Summer Associate - Operational Transaction Services	3/9/13, 5:22 AM
9	Julio J.		nail.com	EY	Senior Consultant	3/1/17, 4:16 PM
10	Bastiaan		mail.com	EY	RPA Manager (BluePrism & UiPath)	7/22/14, 5:23 PM
11	Melvin		@ey.com	EY	CBS Talent Acquisition	2/27/13, 12:25 PM
12	Damayanti		@yahoo.co.in	EY	Assistant Director - Transaction Advisory	1/10/18, 5:46 AM
13	Zachary		@gmail.com	EY	Senior, FSO Advisory	2/11/18, 6:44 AM
14	Jon-Paul		?ey.com	EY	EFS Technology and Operations Leader, Associate Director	12/31/16, 6:01 AM
15	Matt		ski@ey.com	EY	Assistant Director, U.S Transaction Advisory Services Recruiting	9/19/16, 7:55 AM
16	Francesco		il.com	EY	Partner	9/27/17, 5:56 AM
17	Ariel		?hotmail.com	EY	Associate Director - Share Service Center People Advisory Service - Argentina	8/29/16, 5:45 AM

Just start to imagine what you can do. Instead of searching through thousands of connections, looking to see if any of your connections work at your target companies. Pivoting on your connections like this quickly gives you the information you need.

While pivoting on a Company can be valuable, pivoting on position can also be worthwhile.

As we did before, with the Excel file Open > click 'Command' – A (ctrl-A for PC's) to select all of the data. Click 'Insert' > 'Pivot Table.' The image below appears > click 'OK.'

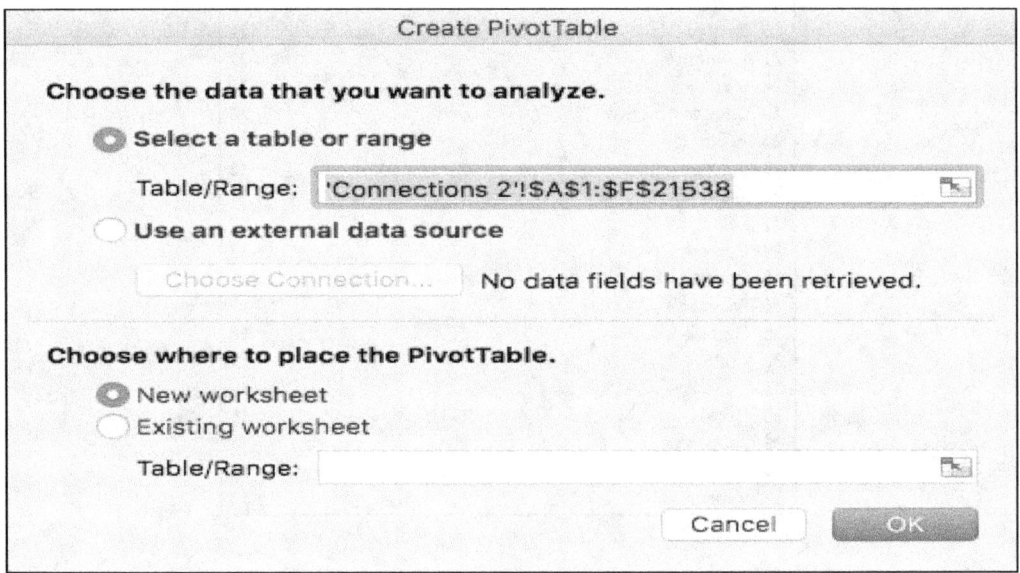

After clicking 'OK,' the new worksheet will contain the following two tables:

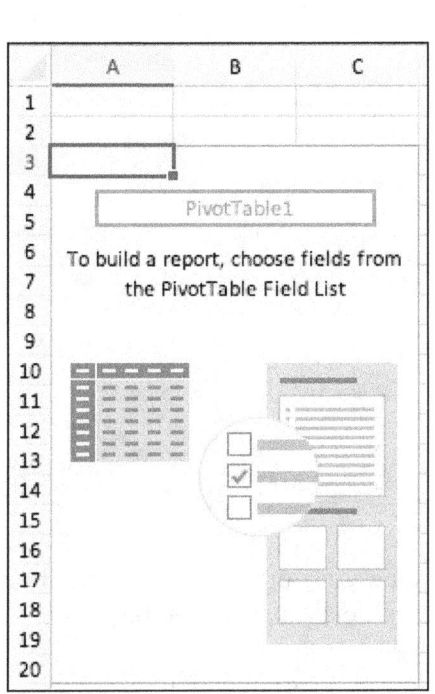

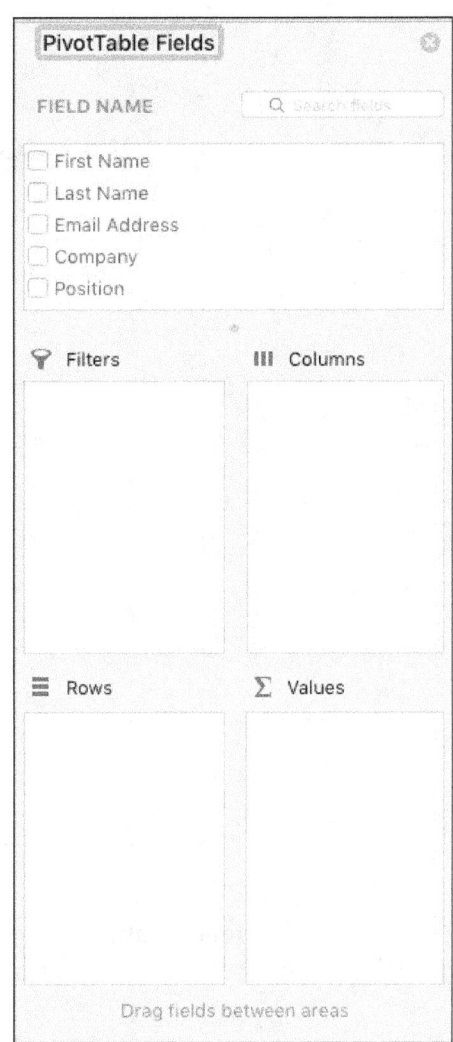

Move the 'Position' field to the 'Rows' section > Move 'Last Name' to the 'Values' section. (If it says 'Sum,' right click on it > click 'Field settings' and choose 'Summarize by Count.'

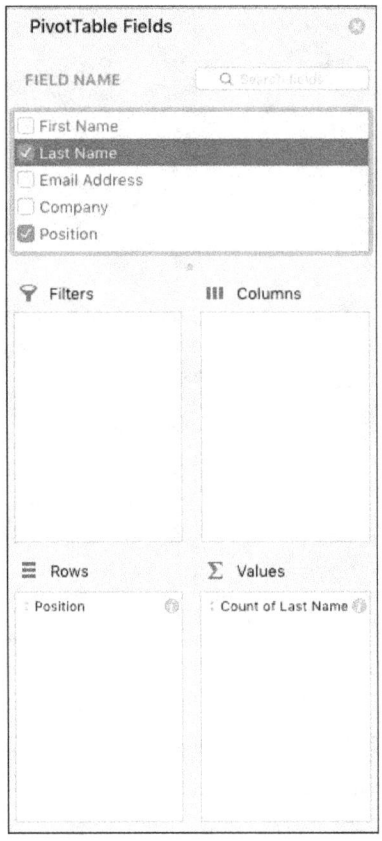

Next, go to the newly created table on the left > place your cursor in column B under the 'Count' column > Right click > 'Sort' > 'Sort Largest to Smallest,' as you see below.

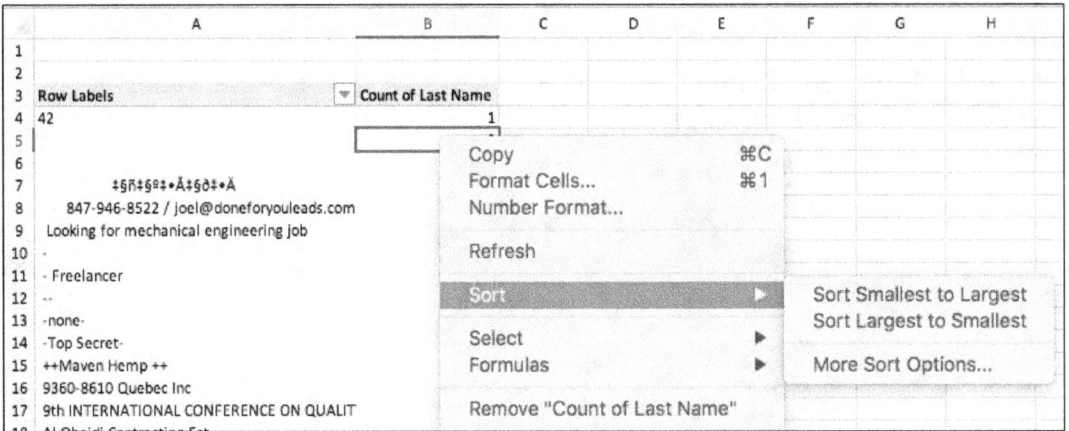

After you follow the steps above, your pivot table will look something like the one below. Again, I've intentionally included a large portion of my pivot table so you can start to see the value.

Row Labels	Count of Last Name
3 Row Labels	Count of Last Name
4 Owner	438
5 CEO	376
6 President	294
7 Founder	265
8 (blank)	254
9 Managing Director	189
10 Director	180
11 Business Development Manager	113
12 Consultant	107
13 Project Manager	95
14 Managing Partner	94
15 Account Manager	92
16 Partner	89
17 co-Founder	82
18 Chief Executive Officer	82
19 Business Owner	78
20 Principal	76
21 Recruiter	76
22 Manager	65
23 Senior Recruiter	62
24 Sales Manager	61
25 General Manager	59
26 Founder & CEO	59
27 Account Executive	56
28 Senior Consultant	53
29 Vice President	50
30 Operations Manager	48
31 Executive Director	47
32 Marketing Manager	40
33 President & CEO	40
34 Business Development	40
35 Founder and CEO	39
36 Technical Recruiter	38
37 Chief Operating Officer	34
38 Regional Sales Manager	32
39 Director Of Operations	31
40 CEO & Founder	31
41 Business Analyst	31
42 Director of Business Development	31

One way a job seeker can use this data is to say "Historically, I've worked for the 'Director of Business Development' in the past", let's look at the Directors of Business Development to see if they work at any of the companies I'm interested in." Remember, even if a job isn't posted, the Director may know of a position that is opening up.

I double-clicked on the '31' next to 'Director of Business Development' and these results were returned.

	A	B	C	D	E
1	First Name	Last Name	Email Address	Company	Position
2	Kevin			Qualcomm	Director of Business Development
3	Augusto			Portland SEO	Director of Business Development
4	Bryan			iCloud Nexus ,òÅ Workday Experts	Director of Business Development
5	Ronald			TopTec Event Tents	Director of Business Development
6	Chris			JobGates Inc.	Director of Business Development
7	Fran			Dulles Regional Chamber of Commerce	Director of Business Development
8	Amit			conf.	Director of Business Development
9	Ali Bin			Aiyin ,Äì Institute of Virtual Reality	Director of Business Development
10	Michael			ElcOsis, LLC	Director of Business Development
11	Anthony			Glasswall Solutions Limited	Director of Business Development
12	Howard			Paradies Gifts, Inc.	Director of Business Development
13	Steve			Grad Solutions	Director of Business Development
14	Brian			Creative Marketing Alliance	Director of Business Development
15	Jason			Sun Knowledge	Director of Business Development
16	Mark			Westar Energy	Director of Business Development
17	Matt			Trusted Architectural Products	Director of Business Development
18	Jacob			Slickdeals, LLC	Director of Business Development
19	Dave			Solid Machine	Director of Business Development
20	Tracy			Wicked Wendy Nutrients	Director of Business Development
21	Karl			Protocast Inc dba Prototype Casting, Inc.	Director of Business Development
22	Krishna			Caelo Communications	Director of Business Development
23	Garrett			Good Clean Vapes	Director of Business Development
24	Frank			Capital Financing	Director of Business Development
25	Gene			Penem Digital Media	Director of Business Development
26	Julie			Applied OLAP, Inc.	Director of Business Development
27	Robert R.			TransPerfect Legal Solutions	Director of Business Development
28	John			Vizit, LLC	Director of Business Development
29	Brady			Modern Business Associates (MBA)	Director of Business Development
30	Doug			Docutrend Imaging Solutions	Director of Business Development
31	Greg			Dise & Company	Director of Business Development
32	Barry			Consonant Custom Media & Worldventures	Director of Business Development

You could also say I'm interested in getting an informational interview with a Senior Recruiter because I'd like to understand more about a role and, whether it would be a good fit for me.

By double-clicking on the '62' next to 'Senior Recruiter' you'll get the same contact information that you see above for 'Directors of Business Development.'

How Do I Build My LinkedIn Network?

I have been on LinkedIn since 2006. As I write in August 2018, I have 23,000 connections. I haven't worked on my connections for 12 years straight. I've worked on it from time to time. Here are some of the things I've done to grow my network.

Join LinkedIn Groups

School Alumni groups are some of the first places where I recommend joining. You'll find your friends there and it will be easier for you to connect. That's why I'm a member of Wake Forest, Webster University and American University Alumni groups.

There are also many groups for current and former employees of corporations.

Because I want to grow my network, I've joined several LION or LinkedIn Open Networker groups. Members of these group pledge to never mark your invite as SPAM or 'IDK' which is short for I Don't Know You.

If you get too many IDK or SPAM responses, LinkedIn will limit the number of invites you can send, or require you provide an email with every invite you send.

I'm a member of these LinkedIn Open Networker (LION) groups.

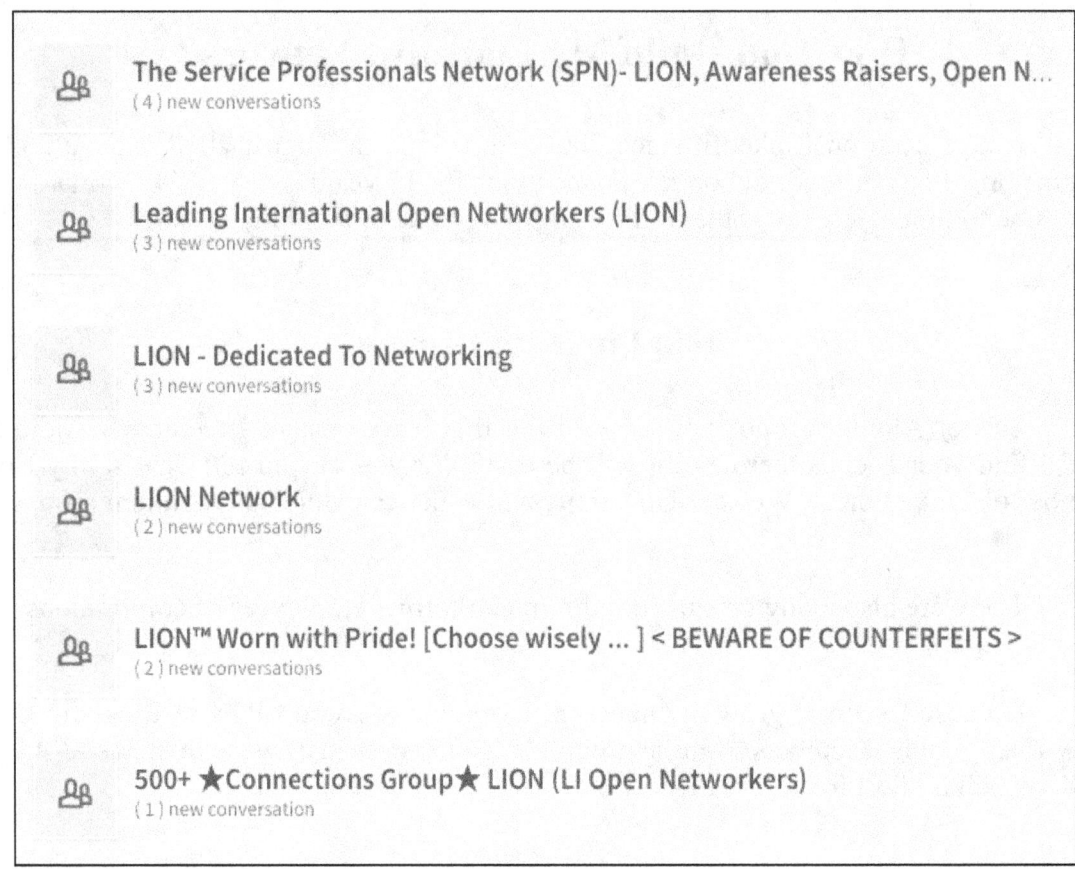

Check Out Your Connections' Groups

It is highly likely your connections belong to groups you will be interested in joining. Check out their groups by going to their profile > scrolling down to their interests > clicking 'See all' and clicking 'Groups' as you see here.

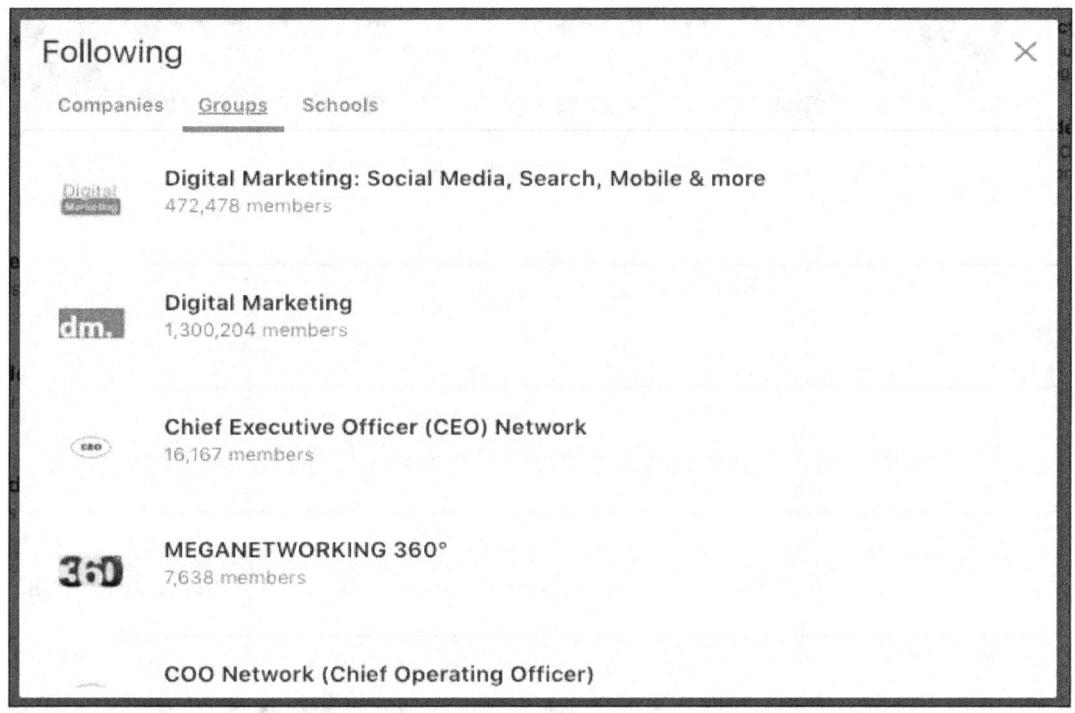

Check Out All of The Groups

Do this by placing your cursor in the LinkedIn search bar, as you see below.

You'll now see these search options. Click on the 'More' drop down and select 'Groups.'

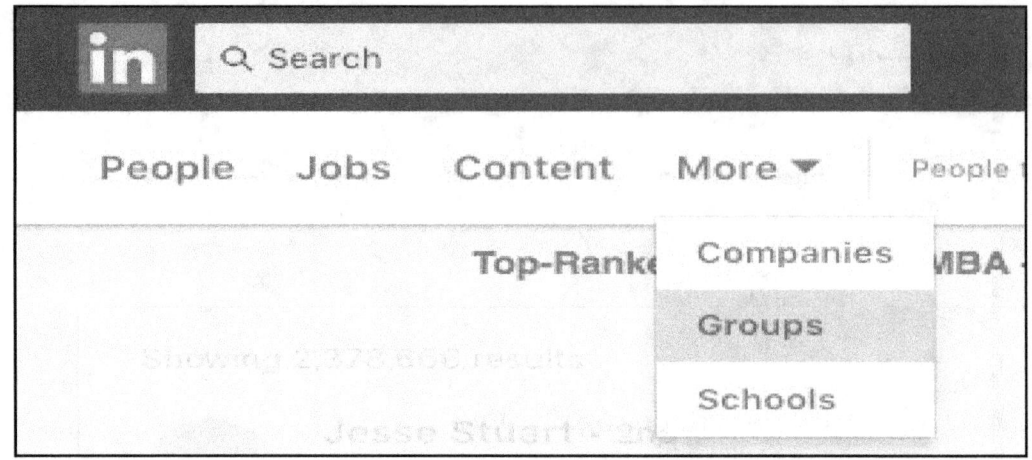

After selecting 'Groups,' you'll see an exhaustive list of LinkedIn groups.

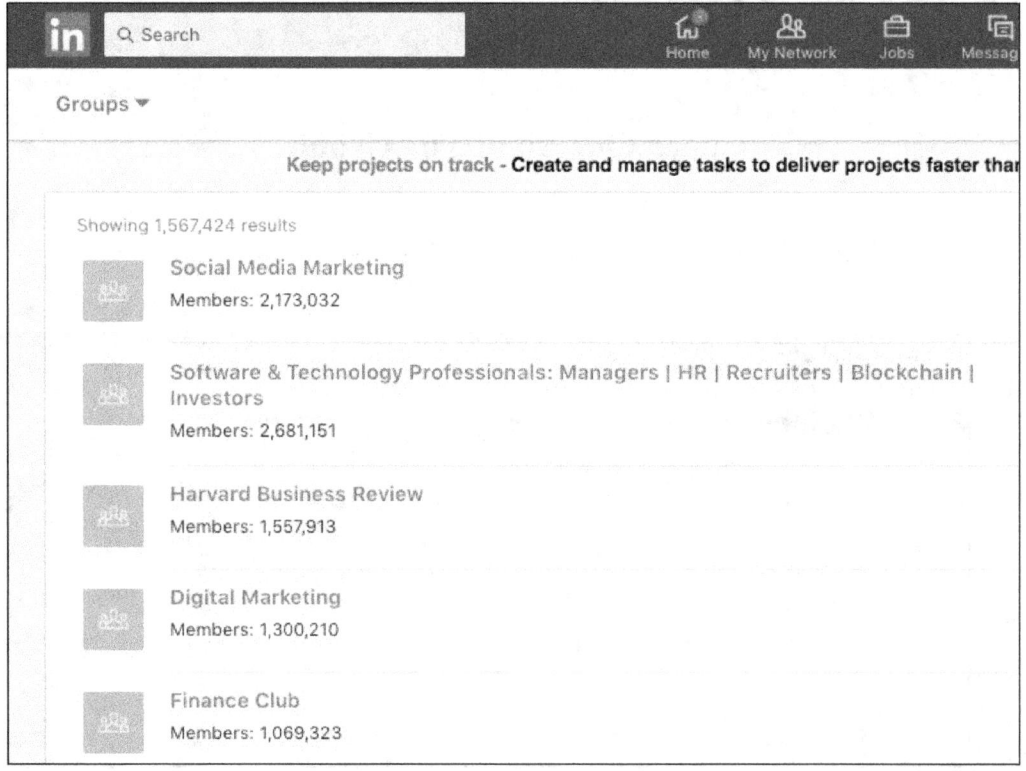

I selected those groups with 'Jobs' in the title and clicked the search magnifying glass. That resulted in the groups you see in the second insert below.

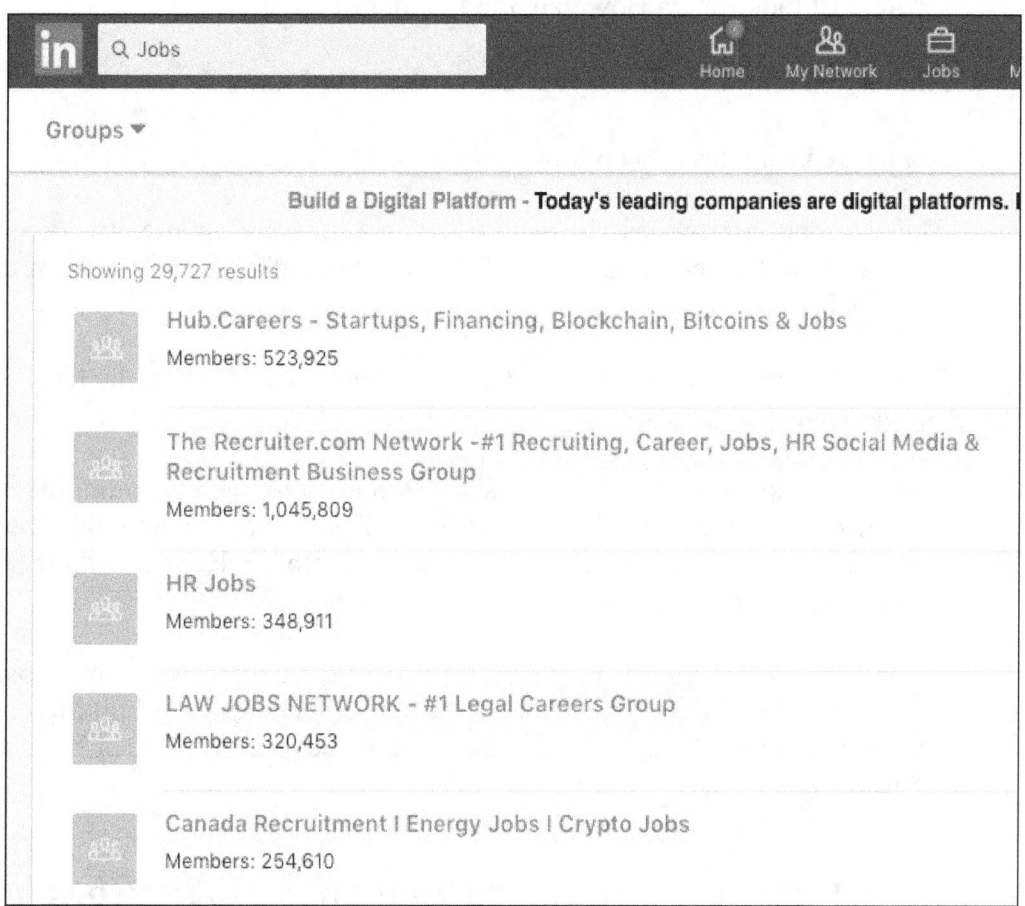

Additional Ways to Build Your Network

- Add 'LION' to your headline to show you're open to invites.

- Prominently state, 'All invites welcome.' You probably don't want to say all invites accepted because there are some you won't want to accept.

- Once you get to 1000 connections or higher, state that in your headline and in the connection requests you send. By taking this step, you are showing the potential connection, 'what's in it for them' if they decide to accept your invite.

- Personalize your connection requests. Wherever possible identify what you share in common, be it connections, groups, employers or schools. At the very least, use their name.

- One of the best LinkedIn groups for growing your network is Project Help You Grow. Just look for Ira Bowman, the founder of the group.

- Another option for building your network is 'TopLinked.'

TopLinked.com has two options:

The free option provides you with a list of LinkedIn Open Networkers that you can upload to LinkedIn. (By doing this you are sending invites to all of the people on the list.)

The paid option, which costs $50.00 a year puts your name on the list. As a result, people send you invites.

Special thanks to author and speaker Donna Serdula for reminding me about TopLinked. Donna shared how she used TopLinked to add on average, one thousand new connections every month! Here's their website: http://www.toplinked.com/.

I also have used TopLinked. Because I do not remember whether I chose the free or paid membership and have used a variety of techniques to build my network, I cannot determine the specific number of connections which can be attributed to TopLinked.

A Final Note on Building Your LinkedIn Network

I could write a book describing the various methods I've used to build my LinkedIn network; hence this section is just a short list of techniques you can use.

Keep in mind, that almost all recruiters have premium LinkedIn memberships, which enable them to search far beyond their personal networks.

Hence, you don't need to build your LinkedIn network so that recruiters can find you.

Where you do need to grow your connections is if you're interested in networking your way into another company, or if you want to reach out to a recruiter.

In addition, LinkedIn groups provide a great way for you to network and connect with folks in your industry. LinkedIn groups also make it possible for you to demonstrate your expertise so that others are more interested in connecting with you.

Is the Job Seeker Premium Membership Worth It?

Every time I've been in the job market, I've purchased The Job seeker Premium Membership for these reasons:

You're Moved to The Top of The Hiring Manager's List

Job Seeker Premium members apply to jobs as a 'Featured Applicant.' As a result, your application appears above job applications from non-Premium members.

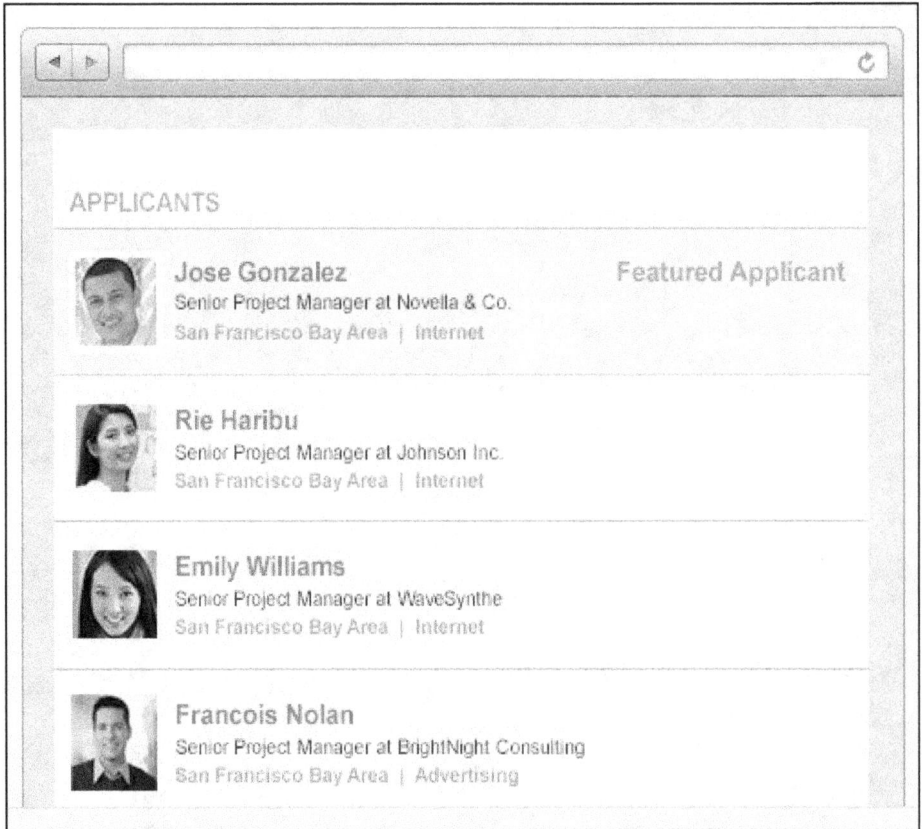

You Can Reach Any Hiring Manager or Recruiter on LinkedIn

Job seeker Premium provides 3 'InMail' credits per month.

InMail enables you to contact anyone on LinkedIn, whether you're connected or not.

With InMail, you can follow up on job applications, set up informational interviews, or make new industry contacts, even when you're not connected.

According to LinkedIn, InMail is 2x more effective than emails or cold calls because it's tied to your LinkedIn profile. Also, if you don't get a response, you're not out one credit.

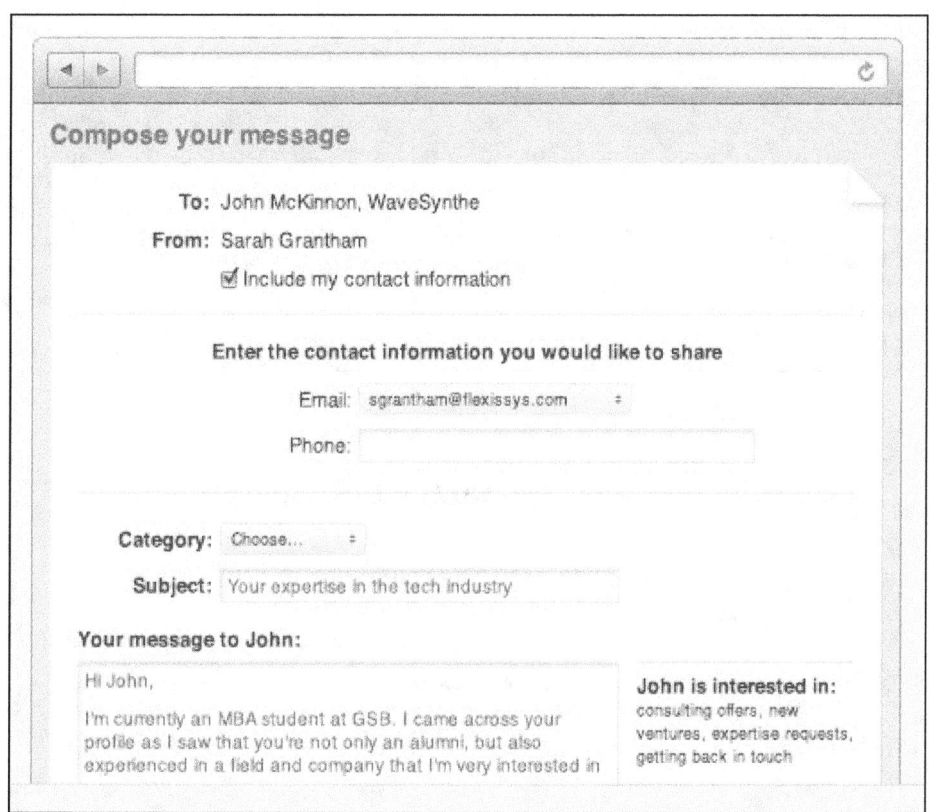

You Can See How You Compare to Other Applicants

Competitive intelligence shows how you compare to other applicants based on skills, education and, seniority. See insert below.

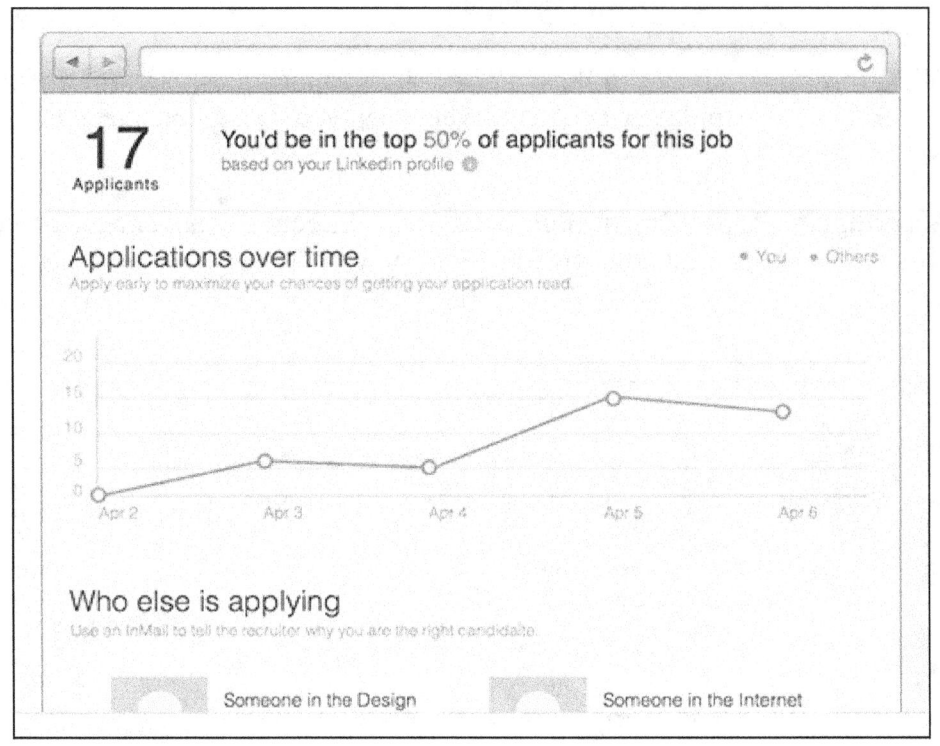

You Get Great Salary Information

See an example of the type of data available below.

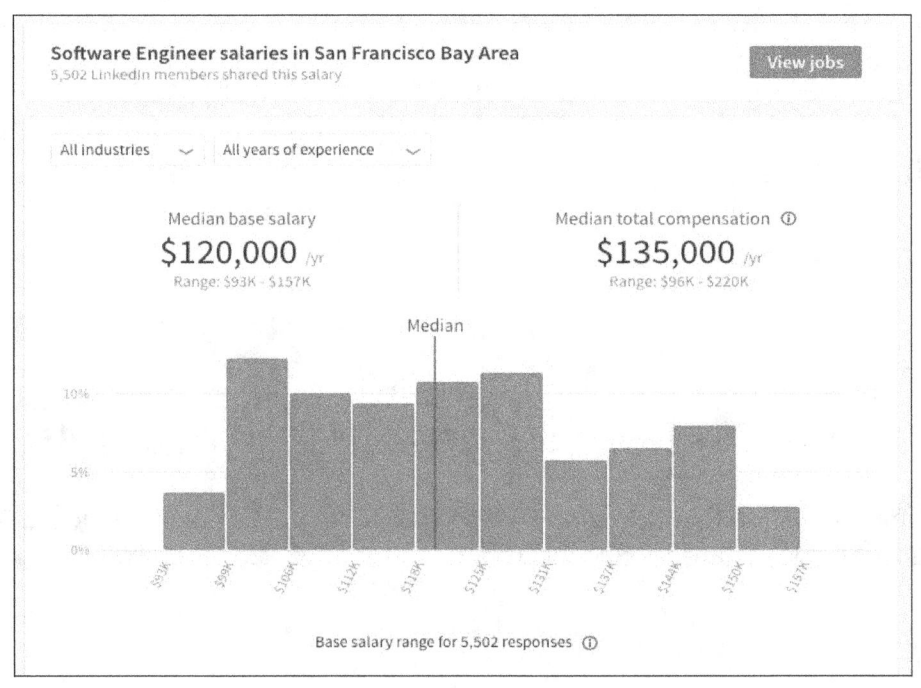

Additional Compensation

Compensation type	Median amount	Range (min - max)	
Annual bonus 44% of respondents reported this	$12,500/yr	$5K	$26K
Sign-on bonus 19% of respondents reported this	$15,000	$5K	$40K
RSUs ⓘ 33% of respondents reported this	$30,000/yr	$5K	$102K
Stock options ⓘ 10% of respondents reported this	$10,000/yr	$2K	$80K

You Can Build Your Skill Set

One of the most appealing parts of the Job seeker Premium Membership is 'LinkedIn Learning.' LinkedIn Learning has 4000+ on-demand business, tech and creative courses taught by leading Industry experts.

One way to stand out in your next interview is to become more valuable by learning new skills. LinkedIn Learning can help. The insert below highlights some of the more popular classes.

Business	Creative	Technology
Business Software	3D and Animation	Data Science
Digital Lifestyle	Art and Illustration	Game Design and Development
Education and Instructional Design	Audio and Music	IT Infrastructure
Finance and Accounting	CAD	Information Management
Leadership + Management	Graphic Design	Software Development
Marketing	Motion Graphics and VFX	User Experience
Professional Development	Photography	Web Design
Project Management	Video	Web Development
Writing		

My Personal Story

Years ago, I made the mistake of asking a so-called 'expert' if I needed the Job seeker membership. He said, "It's not necessary." (He said that because he wanted the money.) When his program produced no results, I signed up for the Job seeker membership and received six calls from recruiters within two weeks!

A Quick Note about LinkedIn Posts

As you use LinkedIn, more and more, you will see a great variety of articles.

Keep in mind, just because someone has written a post in LinkedIn, it doesn't mean you should make decisions based on *that* post.

Here's why I say this:

Years ago, someone wrote a post stating MBAs are not worth your time or money.

I was not pleased because of my own personal experience and I was concerned others may make life decisions based on this post.

I worked for a company where everyone in the Finance department, who did not have an MBA, was laid off.

I have read several articles from 'career experts' where I totally disagree with their advice.

Here's why these articles are written:

Every individual you will meet in your life believes their unique life experiences represent what everyone else will experience in their lives.

Here are some examples:

- I just read a post where someone said, "If you're unhappy with your current role talk to HR about it."

  While every company is different, at many firms whatever an employee communicates to HR is immediately shared with their supervisor.

- During the great recession, when I was in between roles, I messaged a former co-worker and asked her about jobs in the Tampa Bay area.

  She replied, "There are no jobs in Tampa Bay."

  She was obviously misinformed because I had a phone interview for a position in Tampa Bay, the next day.

- I saw this continuously when I was a job seeker. I'd call a friend working for a great company and ask him, "Do you know of any good job opportunities at your company?"

  He responded, "Oh no, they've been eliminating jobs for years."

  After hanging up, I went to his employer's career site and found page upon page of good jobs, many of which I could apply for!

Here's something else for you to chew on. Let's say you're interested in working for company X.

You tell a friend and they respond, "Don't even bother. I went to all of the trouble of applying and preparing for the interview only to get shot down."

After hearing this, keep in mind, everyone is different.

Your friend may have struck out because he couldn't prove that he could do the job; the hiring manager did not believe he'd like the job long enough to stay there; the hiring manager thought her team would not like working with him, or there was a better candidate.

These are just a few of the reasons he could have struck out. Just because, he struck out, doesn't mean that you will strike out.

It is in your moments of decision that your destiny is shaped.

~ Tony Robbins

To Your Success...

LinkedIn Is A Gift to All Job Seekers

Keep this in mind and make the most of your LinkedIn profile. Remember:

'Getting Found' tells the Recruiter you exist.

'The right photo' communicates the impression you want to send.

'A well-crafted headline' quickly communicates your distinct value as a potential employee.

'A well-written summary' tells the Recruiter why they should continue to read your profile.

'A well-thought-out experience section' leaves out none of your accomplishments and, in so doing enables the Recruiter to see why she should call you.

'Career Changing' recommendations from former and current supervisors in your profile will remove any doubt in the Recruiter's mind as to why they should call you.

These 'Career Changing' recommendations can then be used in cover letters that will convert to interviews.

These 'Career Changing' recommendations can also be used in the Summary section of your LinkedIn profile.

Finally, these 'Career' Changing' recommendations can be used in the portfolio you share with the Hiring Manager in your interview.

In addition, now you know how to unlock the power of your existing connections.

If you haven't read Job Hunting Secrets (from someone who's been there), I strongly recommend it!

Be on the lookout for my upcoming book on 'Interviewing Success.'

Successful Job Hunting,

Clark

Would You Be Kind Enough to Write A Quick Amazon Review?

It can be done in 3 minutes – Really, I've done it.

If so, please let others know by following these steps to add your review.

1. Enter www.amazon.com in the URL field.

2. Enter the book title in Amazon's search field.

3. Click on the stars under my name. If there are no reviews yet, scroll down (about half-way) until you see Customer reviews.

4. Click on the 'Write a customer review' button.

If you have suggestions, please tell me.

cfinnical@gmail.com

Be on the lookout for my books on

Interviewing Success

and

Advancing Your Career

Thank you!

Career Coaches...

Two lines hardly do justice to the talent below. I encourage you to go to their websites to find out more:

Patricia Edwards – Career Wisdom Coach –

Patricia's experience as a Talent Manager where she selected thousands of job candidates at top companies puts her in an ideal position to advise and coach job seekers.

https://careerwisdomcoach.com/author/careerwisdomcoach/

Matt Krumrie – Resumes, Career Advice and Job Search Tips –

Matt has authored 2000+ career and job search articles for the Minneapolis Star Tribune, Ziprecruiter.com, CollegeRecruiter.com and Flexjobs.com.

http://www.resumesbymatt.com/

Karen Bartoszek – Salt & Life Coaching, Mentoring, Consulting –

Karen has 25 + years in sales, business development and consulting experience with IBM and AT&T. She also belongs to the International Coaching Federation of Central Florida.

https://www.saltandlifecoach.com/

Kristin A. Sherry – Virtus Career Consulting –

Kristin is a career consultant, speaker and the author of two books, 'Follow Your Star: Career Lessons I Learned from Mom' & '5 Surprising Steps to Land the Job NOW!'

https://virtuscareers.com/

Paula Asinof – Yellow Brick Path –

Paula's background includes 10 years of Executive Search recruiting and Director of Career Services for Sanford-Brown College among other things.

http://www.yellowbrickpath.com/

Liz Ryan – The Human Workplace –

Liz's articles are published in Forbes. She frequently appears on national news networks. Liz Ryan was a corporate HR VP forever. She has a great website.

http://www.humanworkplace.com/

Lisa Rangel – Chameleon Resumes –

Lisa has an amazing amount of valuable information on her website. She has also been the Expert Moderator for LinkedIn's Premium Career Group since 2012.

http://chameleonresumes.com/

Susan P. Joyce – For Smarter Job Search –

Susan has shown us how to identify the correct title for a role when many titles are being used. She also has a wealth of free information on her website.

https://www.job-hunt.org/

Hannah Morgan – Career Sherpa –

Hannah's experience in HR, Outplacement, Workforce Development and Career Services gives her an excellent 360-degree view of job search.

http://careersherpa.net/

Keeping the Faith...

Scriptures I Prayed While Unemployed

Personal note - when everything is ripped away from you and all you have is your faith, you cling all the harder to that faith. Through one merger, two spin-offs, four restructures, and two bosses who tried to fire me, my faith grew more and more, as I saw God carry me through difficult times and answer my prayers.

The LORD is my shepherd, I shall not be in want. He makes me lie down in green pastures, he leads me beside quiet waters, he restores my soul. He guides me in paths of righteousness for his name's sake. Even though I walk through the valley of the shadow of death, I will fear no evil, for you are with me; your rod and your staff, they comfort me. You prepare a table before me in the presence of my enemies. You anoint my head with oil; my cup overflows. Surely goodness and love will follow me all the days of my life, and I will dwell in the house of the LORD forever.

Psalm 23:1-6

And we know that in all things God works for the good of those who love him, who have been called according to his purpose.

Romans 8:28 (NIV)

Trust in the Lord with all your heart and lean not on your own understanding; in all your ways submit to him, and he will make your paths straight.

Proverbs 3:5-6 (NIV)

For I am the Lord your God who takes hold of your right hand and says to you, do not fear; I will help you.

Isaiah 41:13 (NIV)

God is our refuge and strength, an ever-present help in trouble.

Psalm 46:1 (NIV)

He gives strength to the weary and increases the power of the weak.

Isaiah 40:29

So do not fear, for I am with you; do not be dismayed, for I am your God. I will strengthen you and help you; I will uphold you with my righteous right hand.

Isaiah 41:10 (NIV)

I can do all things through him who strengthens me.

Philippians 4:13 (ESV)

For God gave us not a spirit of fearfulness; but of power and love and discipline.

2 Tim 1:7 (ASV)

Ask and it will be given to you; seek and you will find; knock and the door will be opened to you.

Matthew 7:7

Acknowledgements

Special thanks go to HB, DC and CH for their patience while I wrote this book.

In addition, special thanks go to Liam Parfitt for editing my book.

Footnotes

Your vision

[1] I discuss and explain Achievement Stories at length in Job Hunting Secrets (from someone who's been there)

[2] Portfolios will be discussed at length in my third book. In the interim, you can find more information here https://www.linkedin.com/pulse/portfolio-says-superior-candidate-clark-finnical-mba/

How this book will help you

[1] LinkedIn Statistics https://news.linkedin.com/about-us#statistics (Accessed 8-4-2018.)

Your LinkedIn Photo, After Getting Found, Nothing Is More Important

[1] Christine Georghiou. The 7 Factors That Increase The Psychological Impact of Your LinkedIn Profile Photo https://www.yesware.com/blog/best-photo-linkedin/ (Accessed 6-24-2018.)

[2] The Ladders. You Only Get 6 Seconds. https://www.theladders.com/career-advice/you-only-get-6-seconds-of-fame-make-it-count (Accessed 6-24-2018.)

What Do You Have To Say For Yourself – Your Headline

[1] Jane and Tom's LinkedIn Headlines are from Jenny Foss's excellent post, How To Make Your LinkedIn Headline Stand Out which was published in Forbes. https://www.forbes.com/sites/dailymuse/2012/08/14/does-your-linkedin-headline-suck/#2fc5fd3e9335 (Accessed 8-15-2018.)

[2] According to an eye-tracking study by The Ladders, Recruiters spend six seconds on average looking at a resume. LinkedIn profiles get even less time. http://time.com/4403286/linkedin-tips/ (Accessed 6-24-2018.)

[3] Pete Leibman. Please Change Your LinkedIn Headline Now. Here's Why and How. June 11, 2014. https://www.linkedin.com/pulse/20140611214034-7483005-please-change-your-linkedin-headline-now-here-s-why-and-how. (Accessed 6-24-2018.)

[4] Andrew Hutchinson. How to Write the Best LinkedIn Headline (And Why It Matters). Firebrand Ideas Ignition Blog. http://blog.firebrandtalent.com/2015/04/how-to-write-the-best-linkedin-headline-and-why-it-matters/ (Accessed 6-24-2018.)

[5] Ibid.
[6] Ibid. Liebman.
[7] Ibid.
[8] Ibid.
[9] Ibid.

[10] Liz Ryan. How to Write A Killer LinkedIn Headline. Forbes http://www.forbes.com/sites/lizryan/2015/04/10/how-to-write-a-killer-linkedin-headline/2/#9e7a9e449816 (Accessed 6-24-2018.)

[11] Ibid. Liebman.

Does Your Experience Section Generate Interviews?

[1] Huabin Xie, works at Shenzhen, China. **What are the names of the keyboard symbols?** https://www.quora.com/What-are-the-names-of-the-keyboard-symbols (Accessed 6-24-2018.)

[2] Another helpful resource is Katharine Hansen's. You Are More Accomplished Than You Think: How to Brainstorm Your Achievements for Career and Life Success Quintessential Careers Press. Kindle Edition.

LinkedIn Recommendations Can Lead To Your Dream Job

[1] Jessica Smith. How to Give — and Get — LinkedIn Recommendations. Resume Butterfly. http://resumebutterfly.com/how-to-give-and-get-linkedin-recommendations/ (Accessed 6-24-2018)

[2] The Truth About LinkedIn Endorsements: https://www.mjsearch.com/the-truth-about-linkedin-endorsements/ (Accessed 8-4-2018.)

[3] Aline Lerner, "LinkedIn endorsements are dumb. Here's the data." Interviewing.io blog http://blog.interviewing.io/linkedin-endorsements-are-dumb-heres-the-data/ (Accessed 8-4-2018.)

[4] Joseph Liu. Get LinkedIn recommendations instead of endorsements. https://www.thedrum.com/opinion/2014/03/19/get-linkedin-recommendations-instead-endorsements (Accessed 8-4-2018.)

Are You Taking Advantage Of Everything You Can Do With Your Name?

[1] Scott Singer. 4 Easy Hacks To Help You Get Noticed on LinkedIn. https://www.linkedin.com/pulse/4-easy-hacks-help-get-you-noticed-linkedin-scott?trk=hp-feed-article-title-publish (Accessed 6-24-2018.)

[2] Nicola Fairweather. How to Add a Professional Designation to Your LinkedIn Name. https://www.linkedin.com/pulse/how-add-credentials-your-linkedin-profile-name-nicola-fairweather-ba?trk=mp-reader-card (Accessed 6-24-2018.)

Is Your Education Section Helping Or Hurting?

[1] The Muse. Your Handy Answer To 'How Long Do I Keep My Graduation Year on My Resume?' June 7, 2017. https://www.forbes.com/sites/dailymuse/2017/06/07/your-handy-answer-to-how-long-do-i-keep-my-graduation-year-on-my-resume/#7e6104a86d2e (Accessed 6-25-2018.)

Spicing Up Your LinkedIn Profile

[1] Brynne Tillman, Symbols to spice up your LinkedIn profile. https://www.linkedin.com/pulse/20140423001152-22901019-symbols-to-spice-up-your-linkedin-profile/ (Accessed 8-4-2018.)

[2] Ibid.

With LinkedIn You Can Search, Apply and Learn When Jobs Are Posted

[1] Rob Dalton. Getting Ghosted On Your Job Applications? Here's Fix #1: Apply Within 96 Hours Sept 28, 2017. https://talent.works/blog/2017/09/28/getting-ghosted-on-your-job-applications-heres-fix-1-apply-within-96-hours/?utm_content=bufferf5d4a&utm_medium=social&utm_source=plus.google.com&utm_campaign=buffer (Accessed 6-24-2018.)